AN ADAPTED CLASSIC

Macbeth

William Shakespeare

GLOBE FEARON
Pearson Learning Group

Project Editor: Kristen Shepos-Salvatore
Editorial Supervisor: Cary Pepper
Editorial Assistant: Kathleen Kennedy
Production Editor: Alan Dalgleish
Marketing Manager: Sandra Hutchison
Art Supervision: Patricia Smythe
Electronic Page Production: Luc Van Meerbeek
Illustrator and Cover Illustration: Thomas Sperling

ISBN: 0-835-91854-8
Printed in the United States of America

5 6 7 8 9 10 11   05 04 03 02

Globe
Fearon

Pearson Learning Group

1-800-321-3106
www.pearsonlearning.com

CONTENTS

ABOUT THE AUTHOR

There are many things we do not know for certain about William Shakespeare. It is believed he was born on April 26, 1564. He grew up in Stratford upon Avon, a small town in England. He married Anne Hathaway in 1582, when he was 18. They had three children, two girls and one boy. Shakespeare went to London, where he became successful as an actor, a playwright, and a poet. He belonged to a group of actors called The King's Men, who performed his plays. In 1599, The King's Men built a theater, which they named the Globe. The Globe became one of the best-known theaters in London. Shakespeare's plays were also performed at court, for Queen Elizabeth I and King James I. Shakespeare retired from the theater around 1613. He returned to Stratford, where he bought a house and land. William Shakespeare died on April 23, 1616. He is buried in Stratford.

Who really wrote Shakespeare's plays is one of literature's great mysteries. Some people say that one man could not have written so many excellent plays. Some people think that if one man did write them, it was not Shakespeare, because they believe he was poorly educated. Other people say he did write the plays that bear his name, and consider William Shakespeare the world's greatest playwright.

PREFACE

Macbeth is the shortest play Shakespeare wrote. The play was probably written as a tribute to King James I of England. It was first performed for James I in 1606. Shakespeare knew that the king had a great interest in the supernatural. That might explain why the supernatural is so important in the play.

In *Macbeth* we see a flattering portrayal of the origins of the Stuart line, a branch of the royal family of which James I was a part. In fact, Banquo, one of the characters in the play, was a real-life ancestor of James I. But in real life, he was not as good as Shakespeare makes him in the play. This play is a story about ambition, fear, and guilt. It is also the story of how these things can affect people's lives.

ADAPTER'S NOTE

In preparing this edition of *Macbeth,* we have kept as closely as possible to William Shakespeare's original words. We have changed some of the vocabulary. We have also shortened and simplified some scenes and lines. Some of the footnotes will make the language clearer. Other footnotes will provide more historical detail. None of the story has been left out.

HISTORICAL BACKGROUND

Shakespeare's most productive years were during what is called the Elizabethan Age in England. During the years of Elizabeth I's reign (1558-1603), theatrical drama was very important. This period is also known as the English Renaissance. London's first public theater was built in 1576 by James Burbage. It was so popular that by 1585 a second playhouse was being used.

Shakespeare's London was a busy medieval city. It was the center of England's social, business, and intellectual life. It was the only city in England that was fully under the influence of the Renaissance (the flowering of art and culture in Italy, France, and Spain). Most of the printing and publishing in England was done in London. In England, theaters for the public performance of drama were found only in London. London, in short, was the heart of England. In the sense that he pumped new life into London's cultural scene, Shakespeare was the heart of London.

Shakespeare based *Macbeth* on a story from Holinshed's *Chronicles,* a history of England, Scotland, and Ireland. He followed the original story very closely, but he changed a few details. In the original story, for example, Macbeth had been ruling for ten years before he ordered the murders of Banquo and Fleance. Another difference is that in Holinshed's story, Banquo helped in the killing of Duncan. Shakespeare gave a more flattering portrait of Banquo than Holinshed did. The reason for this was probably that he was trying to flatter James I, who was related to Banquo.

Elizabethan Theater

Theaters in Shakespeare's time were designed very differently from modern theaters. The stage jutted out into the audience. It took up the space now used by the first few rows of seats. This stage had no curtain to be raised, lowered, or opened. There were hardly any stage props. Sets were very simple. In fact, the audience had to use their imagination a great deal. For them, the same set might have to work as a street scene or a ballroom scene.

The rear of the stage had a small curtained area. This could be used as an inner room, a tomb, or a prison. There were balconies on the sides of the stage. These were used for upper decks of ships, balconies of houses, and prison windows.

When theaters were not available, plays were performed in public places, such as inns and taverns. This is one reason Elizabethan plays had so many speeches that could be delivered in loud voices. The playwright had to make sure the audience could hear everything.

These are just some of the physical differences between Elizabethan theater and today's theater. There is also another important difference. Women were not allowed to act. All parts were played by men. Most women's roles were played by boys. They were often recruited from the boys' choirs in London churches.

CAST OF CHARACTERS

DUNCAN	The good and honest King of Scotland
MALCOLM	Duncan's older son
DONALBAIN	Duncan's younger son
MACBETH	The main character of the play. When the story opens, he is a captain in Duncan's army.
LADY MACBETH	Macbeth's wife
BANQUO	A nobleman, a captain in Duncan's army, and Macbeth's friend.
FLEANCE	Banquo's son
MACDUFF	A nobleman
LADY MACDUFF	Macduff's wife
MACDUFF'S SON	A young boy

LENNOX
ANGUS
ROSS } Scottish noblemen
MENTEITH
CAITHNESS

OLD SIWARD	Earl of Northumberland
YOUNG SIWARD	The son of Old Siward
SEYTON	Macbeth's lieutenant
THE THREE WITCHES	
PORTER	Keeper of Macbeth's castle
THREE MURDERERS	
CAPTAIN	An officer in Duncan's army
OLD MAN	
DOCTOR	
GENTLEWOMAN	A servant of Lady Macbeth
BANQUO'S GHOST	
ATTENDANTS	
MESSENGERS	
SERVANTS	
LORDS	
VISIONS	

Act 1

Scene 1

A heath.[1] Thunder and lightning. Three WITCHES *enter.*

WITCH 1: When shall we three meet again
   In thunder, lightning, or in rain?

WITCH 2: When the hurlyburly's done,
   When the battle's lost and won.

WITCH 3: Before the setting of the sun.

WITCH 1: Where shall we meet?

WITCH 2: Upon the heath.

WITCH 3: There we will meet Macbeth.

ALL: Fair is foul, and foul is fair.
   Hover through the fog and filthy air.

(ALL *exit.*)

Scene 2

A camp near Forres. KING DUNCAN, MALCOLM, DONALBAIN, LENNOX, *and* ATTENDANTS *enter. They meet a bleeding* CAPTAIN.

DUNCAN: What bloody man is that?
   He can tell us how the battle is going.

MALCOLM: This is the man
   Who, like a good and strong soldier, fought
   To keep me from being captured.
   Hail, brave friend!
   Tell the King what was happening on the battlefield

---

1. **heath**   a large area of level, open land

When you left it.

CAPTAIN: At one point, it seemed doubtful,
Like two tired swimmers that cling together
And pull each other down. The rebel forces
Seemed to be swarming upon Macbeth,
But they were too weak for him.
Brave Macbeth—
And he well deserves that description—
Took out his sword and carved his passage
Through the enemy forces till he faced his foe.
Without shaking hands, or bidding farewell to him,
Macbeth cut him through from navel to jaws,
And then placed his head upon our battlements.[2]

DUNCAN: Oh, brave cousin! Worthy gentleman!

CAPTAIN: But just as the battle seemed to be
Going our way,
New dangers came from the east.
Listen, King of Scotland, listen!
The Norwegian lord,
Hoping to gain an advantage,
With fresh weapons and new supplies of men
Began a fresh assault.

DUNCAN: Did this not dismay
Our captains, Macbeth and Banquo?

CAPTAIN: Yes;
About as much as sparrows dismay eagles,
Or hares dismay lions.
To tell you the truth, I must report that they were
Like cannons with extra heavy charges.

---

2. battlements high parts of castle walls, with openings, used
in defense

For each enemy stroke, they gave two times two.
Whether they meant to bathe in their own blood,
Or make the battleground famous for their fight,
I cannot tell.
But I am faint, my wounds cry for help.

DUNCAN: Your words and your wounds
Have this much in common:
They both tell of your honor.
(*to the* ATTENDANTS) Go get him surgeons.

(CAPTAIN *exits, attended.* ROSS *and* ANGUS *enter.*)

Who comes here?

MALCOLM: The worthy Thane[3] of Ross.

ROSS: God save the King!

DUNCAN: Where did you come from, worthy Thane?

ROSS: From Fife, great king,
Where the Norwegian flags fill the sky
And chill our men with fear.
The King of Norway himself, with many soldiers,
Began a terrible battle.
He was assisted by that most disloyal traitor,
The Thane of Cawdor.
Finally, Macbeth, dressed in armor,
Showed strength equal to his own.
At last, the victory fell on us!

DUNCAN: Great happiness!

ROSS: Now Sweno, Norway's king,
Wants to surrender.
He wants to know the terms of peace.
We would not let him bury his men

---

3. Thane   a Scottish lord

Until he paid us 10,000 dollars.

DUNCAN: The Thane of Cawdor shall pay
For his treachery.
Go see to his instant death,
And give his former title to Macbeth.

ROSS: I'll see it done.

DUNCAN: What he has lost, noble Macbeth has won.

(ALL *exit.*)

Scene 3

A heath near Forres. Thunder. The three WITCHES *enter.*

WITCH 1: A drum, a drum!
Macbeth does come.

ALL: The Weird Sisters, hand in hand,
Travelers over the sea and land,
Thus do go about, about;
Three times to yours,
Three times to mine,
And three times more,
To make up nine.
That's enough! The charm's wound up.

(MACBETH *and* BANQUO *enter.*)

MACBETH: So foul and fair a day I have not seen.

BANQUO: How far is it to Forres? (*He sees the* WITCHES.)
What are those creatures, so withered
And wild in their attire?
They do not look like inhabitants of the earth,
And yet they are on it.
Do you live?
Or are you creatures of our imagination?

You seem to understand me,
For you all put your chapped fingers
To your skinny lips at the same time.
You might be women,
And yet your beards forbid me to think
That you are.

MACBETH: Speak, if you can. What are you?

WITCH 1: All hail, Macbeth! Hail to you, Thane of
Glamis!

WITCH 2: All hail, Macbeth! Hail to you, Thane of
Cawdor!

WITCH 3: All hail, Macbeth, who shall be King hereafter!

BANQUO (to MACBETH): Good sir, why do you draw back
And seem to fear things that sound so good?
(to the WITCHES) In the name of truth,
Are you just fantasies, or are you indeed
What you seem to be?
You greet my noble partner
With good news about his future,
Saying that he will have noble possessions
And high rank.
He seems to be in a trance.
Yet you do not speak to me.
If you can look into the future,
And say what will happen and what will not,
Speak then to me, who neither begs nor fears
Your favors or your hate.

WITCH 1: Hail!

WITCH 2: Hail!

WITCH 3: Hail!

WITCH 1: Lesser than Macbeth, and greater.

WITCH 2: Not so happy, yet much happier.

WITCH 3: Your sons and grandsons shall be kings,
Though you will not be one.
So all hail, Macbeth and Banquo!

WITCH 1: Banquo and Macbeth, all hail!

MACBETH: Stay, you imperfect speakers, tell me more.
Since my father's death,
I have been Thane of Glamis,
But how can I be Thane of Cawdor, too?
The Thane of Cawdor still lives,
A well-to-do gentleman, and to be king
Is no more possible than to be Thane of Cawdor.
Tell me how you got this strange information,
And why you stop us on this heath
With such greetings and prophecies.
Speak, I say!

(WITCHES *vanish.*)

BANQUO: The earth has bubbles, as the water does,
And these must be bubbles, too.
Where have they vanished to?

MACBETH: Into the air,
And what seemed real has melted
As breath into the wind.
I wish they had stayed!

BANQUO: Were they really here,
Or has our reason been taken prisoner?

MACBETH: Your children shall be kings.

BANQUO: You shall be King.

MACBETH: And Thane of Cawdor, too;
Isn't that what they said?

BANQUO: They used those very words.
(*He hears a noise.*) Who's there?

(ROSS *and* ANGUS *enter.*)

ROSS: The King has happily received
The news of your success, Macbeth.
He is so astonished by everything you did
On the battlefield that he doesn't know
How to begin to praise you.
He has heard stories from all sides
About your bravery, and he is very pleased.

ANGUS: We have been sent by the King
To tell you that he thanks you.
He wants us to take you to him right away.

ROSS: As advance payment toward greater honors,
He told me to call you Thane of Cawdor,
So I say, Hail, most worthy Thane!
The title is now yours.

BANQUO (*aside*[4]): What?
Did the Witches tell the truth?

MACBETH: The Thane of Cawdor lives.
Why do you dress me in borrowed robes?

ANGUS: He who was the Thane is still alive,
But he has confessed to the crime of treason,[5]
And he has been sentenced to death.

MACBETH (*aside*): Thane of Glamis, and now
Thane of Cawdor, too!

---

4. **aside** a term used in plays to indicate that the speaker's words are meant just for the audience and cannot be heard by any of the other characters
5. **treason** betrayal of one's country or ruler

The greatest title is yet to come!
(*to* ROSS *and* ANGUS) Thanks for your trouble.
(*to* BANQUO) Do you not hope that your children
Shall be kings? After all, those who told me
I would be Thane of Cawdor
Promised such honors to your children.

BANQUO: Those promises, if trusted fully,
Might also excite you to hope for the crown,
In addition to the title of Thane of Cawdor.
But these promises are strange.
Often, to bring great harm to us,
The instruments of evil tell us some truths,
And win us over with small things,
Only to betray us in matters of greater importance.

MACBETH (*to* ROSS *and* ANGUS): I thank you, gentlemen.
(*aside*) This supernatural temptation
Cannot be evil, cannot be good. If evil,
Why has it given me evidence of success
By starting with a truth?
For it is true that I am now Thane of Cawdor.
If good, why do I think that thought
Whose horrid image makes my heart
Knock against my ribs, just to think of it?
These fears are less than horrible daydreams.
My thoughts about murdering the King
Shake me so much that I'm overpowered
By one idea—
To get the crown—
And nothing seems real to me but that.

BANQUO (*to* ROSS *and* ANGUS): Look at how Macbeth
Seems to be in a trance.

MACBETH (*aside*): If it is my fate to be King,

Then fate may crown me
Without any action on my part.

BANQUO (*to* ROSS *and* ANGUS): New honors come to him.
Like new clothes, they will fit better
After they have been used for a while.

MACBETH (*aside*): Come what may,
Time and the hour runs through the roughest day.

BANQUO: Worthy Macbeth, we're waiting.

MACBETH: I'm sorry. My dull brain was full of
Things forgotten. Please forgive me.
Let us go to see the King.
(*to* BANQUO) Think about what has happened,
And when we have more time, let us get together
To talk about it.

BANQUO: Very gladly.

MACBETH: Till then, enough.
Come, friends.

(ALL *exit.*)

Scene 4

Forres. The palace. KING DUNCAN, MALCOLM, DONALBAIN,
LENNOX, *and* ATTENDANTS *enter.*

DUNCAN: Has the Thane of Cawdor been executed yet?

MALCOLM: My lord, I have not heard an official report,
But I have spoken with someone who saw him die.
He said that Cawdor confessed his treasons,
Begged your Highness's pardon,
And said he was very sorry.
Nothing in his life
Was as honorable as his leaving it.

He died as one who had rehearsed well,
And knew how
To throw away the dearest thing he owned,
As if it were a careless trifle.

DUNCAN: There is no way to know what a person
Is really thinking by looking at the face.
He was a gentleman whom I trusted completely.

(MACBETH, BANQUO, ROSS, *and* ANGUS *enter.*)

Dear Macbeth! It is so good to see you!
I hardly know how to thank you.
I owe you more than I could ever pay!

MACBETH: Being able to serve you loyally
Is payment in itself. It is our duty and an honor
To do what we can to keep you safe.

DUNCAN: Welcome! Great honors will soon be yours.
Noble Banquo, you also deserve great honors.
Let me embrace you and hold you to my heart.

BANQUO: It is an honor to serve you, my lord.

DUNCAN: Sons, kinsmen, Thanes,
And all you who are near to me, hear this.
I name as my successor my eldest son, Malcolm.
Hereafter, he shall be called
The Prince of Cumberland.
He is not the only one who will be honored.
Signs of nobleness, like stars, shall shine
On all those who deserve them.
Let us now go to Macbeth's castle at Inverness
For a visit.

MACBETH: I'll go on ahead and tell my wife
The good news.
She will want to prepare for your visit.

I humbly take my leave.

DUNCAN: My worthy Cawdor!

MACBETH (*aside*): The Prince of Cumberland!
   That is a step
   On which I must fall, or jump over,
   For it lies in my way. Stars, hide your fires;
   Do not let light see my black and deep desires.

(MACBETH *exits.*)

DUNCAN: True, worthy Banquo; he is so brave,
   And in his praises I am fed;
   It is a banquet to me. Let's go after him
   Who has gone before us to bid us welcome.
   He is a kinsman without equal.

(ALL *exit.*)

Scene 5

Inverness. Macbeth's castle. MACBETH'S WIFE *enters, alone, with a letter.*

LADY MACBETH (*reading*): "They met me in the day of success, and I have learned that they can predict the future. When I asked them to tell me more, they vanished into the air. While I stood there in a trance, wondering about it, two messengers came from the King. They called me 'Thane of Cawdor,' the same title the three Weird Sisters had used. The Sisters also said, 'Hail, King that shall be!' I thought you would like to hear about this, my dearest partner of greatness. This way, you will not lose any time in rejoicing over the greatness that is promised to you. Hold it to your heart, and farewell."

(*commenting on the letter*) Thane of Glamis you are
   already.
And you are also Thane of Cawdor. You shall be
What you were promised. Yet I do fear your nature;
It is too full of the milk of human kindness
To go the fastest way. You want to be great,
You have ambition, but you are without
The evil that it takes to get what you want.
You would have it through honest means,
But it can only be gotten by evil.
You need someone to say, "You must do this,
If you want that." Hurry home,
So that I may pour my spirit in your ear,
And tell you, with the strength of my own voice,
What stands between you and the golden crown
That fate and the supernatural already seem
To see on your head.

(*A* MESSENGER *enters.*)

What news do you have?

MESSENGER: The King will be coming here tonight.

LADY MACBETH: You are mad to say it!
   Isn't my husband with him? He would have told me
   To prepare for the King's visit.

MESSENGER: May it please you, it is true.
   Our Thane is on his way here. The messenger
   Who brought the news was so out of breath
   From running, that he had only enough left
   To say the news.

LADY MACBETH: Take care of him.
   He brings great news.

(MESSENGER *exits.*)

The raven is hoarse
From croaking about the fatal entrance of Duncan
Under my battlements. Come, you spirits
That go with deadly thoughts,
Fill me from head to toe
With terrible cruelty!
Make my blood thick;
Stop any feelings of remorse and sorrow,
So that no feelings of human nature
May shake my evil purpose.
Come, thick night,
And wrap yourself in the darkest smoke,
So my keen knife will not see the wound it makes,
Nor will heaven peep through
The blanket of the dark
To cry, "Stop! Stop!"

(MACBETH *enters.*)

Great Glamis! Worthy Cawdor!
Greater than both in the near future.
Your letter has carried me beyond
This ignorant present, and I feel now
The future in this very moment.

MACBETH: My dearest love,
Duncan comes here tonight.

LADY MACBETH: And when does he leave?

MACBETH: Tomorrow, according to his plan.

LADY MACBETH: Oh, never shall he see the sun again!
Your face, my husband,
Is like a book where anyone
Can read strange things.
To fool the time, look like the time.

Show welcome in your eye,
Your hand, your words;
Look like the innocent flower,
But be the serpent under it.
He who is coming
Must be taken care of.
You must put
This night's great business into my hands,
And I shall arrange everything.

MACBETH: We will speak further.

LADY MACBETH: Show only calm.
Give no one reasons to be suspicious.
Leave all the rest to me.

(BOTH *exit.*)

Scene 6

Before Macbeth's castle. KING DUNCAN, MALCOLM,
DONALBAIN, BANQUO, LENNOX, MACDUFF, ROSS, ANGUS,
and ATTENDANTS *enter.*

DUNCAN: This castle is in a pleasant place.
The air softly and sweetly appeals
To our gentle senses.

BANQUO: This summer bird, the martin,
Approves of this place, too.
I have noticed that they usually make their nests
In places where the air is delicate.

(LADY MACBETH *enters.*)

DUNCAN: Greetings, our gracious hostess!
I thank you for all the trouble you have gone to
In preparing for our visit.

LADY MACBETH: It is an honor to have you here.

DUNCAN: Where's the Thane of Cawdor?
> We were right behind him, but he rides well,
> And his great love for you, sharp as his spur,
> Helped him to get home well before us.
> Fair and noble hostess,
> We are your guests tonight.

LADY MACBETH: Your servants are always happy
> To have the pleasure of your company.

DUNCAN: Give me your hand, and
> Take me to my host. We love him dearly,
> And shall continue to hold him in high regard.
> By your leave, hostess.

(ALL *exit.*)

Scene 7

Within Macbeth's castle. MACBETH *enters.*

MACBETH: If it must be done, then it's best
> That it be done quickly. If this assassination
> Could just be the end of it, with no consequences,
> That would be fine. Here, on this river of time,
> I would risk the life to come. It is the thought
> Of punishment in the hereafter that stops me.
> Even-handed justice puts the ingredients
> Of our poisoned cups to our own lips.
> Duncan trusts me for several reasons.
> I am his kinsman and his subject.
> I am also his host. I should be shutting the door
> Against his murderer, not holding the knife myself.
> Besides, Duncan is a good man.
> I have no reason to hurt him,

Except my own ambition,
Which, like an eager rider, jumps over the horse,
And falls on the other side.

(LADY MACBETH *enters.*)

Hello! What's the news?

LADY MACBETH: King Duncan is almost finished eating.
Why have you left the room?

MACBETH: Has he asked for me?

LADY MACBETH: Of course he has.

MACBETH: We will go no further in this business.
He has honored me recently, and I have earned
Golden opinions from all sorts of people.
I should wear these now while they are still new,
And not cast them aside so soon.

LADY MACBETH: What about your hopes for the future?
Have they been sleeping? And do they wake now,
Looking pale and weak? Are you afraid
To be the same in your act and courage
As you are in your wishes?
Do you wish to live as a coward in your own eyes,
Not daring to reach for what you want?
You are like the cat who wanted the fish
But was afraid to get its feet wet.

MACBETH: Be quiet, please!
I dare do all that a man can do.
Anyone who would do more is an animal.

LADY MACBETH: What beast was it, then,
That made you break your promise to me?
When you dared to do it, then you were a man;
And, to be more than what you were, you would
Be so much more the man.

I have given milk to a baby, and I know
How tender it is to love the baby that takes it.
Yet I would, while it was smiling in my face,
Have plucked the nipple from his boneless gums
And dashed his brains out, if I had sworn to you
That I would do so.

MACBETH: What if we should fail?

LADY MACBETH: Fail?
Have enough courage to see this through,
And we'll not fail. When Duncan is asleep—
And this day's hard journey will soon see to that—
I'll give his two guards wine and liquor.
They'll soon be asleep, too.
With Duncan unguarded, we can do anything!
How might we make
His drunken guards look guilty
Of our great murder?

MACBETH: After we have marked with blood
Those two sleeping guards,
And used their own daggers
For the crime, everyone will think they did it.

LADY MACBETH: Of course! Who could think otherwise,
Especially when we'll be crying the loudest about
Duncan's death?

MACBETH: Then it's settled. We'll carry out the plan.
Away, and fool the time with fairest show;
False face must hide what false heart does know.

(BOTH *exit.*)

Act 2

Scene 1

The courtyard of Macbeth's castle. BANQUO, FLEANCE, *and a* SERVANT *with a torch enter.*

BANQUO: What time is it, son?

FLEANCE: The moon is down. I have not heard the clock.

BANQUO: And the moon goes down at midnight.

FLEANCE: I guess it must be after midnight, then, sir.

BANQUO: Here, hold my sword.
    There is thriftiness in the heavens;
    All the stars, like candles, have been put out.
    Here, hold my dagger, too. A heavy feeling
    Lies like lead upon me, yet I could not sleep.
    Merciful angels, stop the cursed thoughts
    That keep me awake!

(MACBETH *enters, followed by a* SERVANT *with a torch.* BANQUO *is startled. He speaks first to* FLEANCE.)

    Give me my sword.
    (*He calls out.*) Who's there?

MACBETH: A friend.

BANQUO: What, sir, you're not asleep yet?
    The King's in bed. He was in a good mood,
    And he sent great gifts to your servants' quarters.
    He said that your wife was an excellent hostess,
    And then he went to bed, quite content.

MACBETH: Being unprepared for the King's visit,
    I am afraid that we did not do enough for him.

BANQUO: All was well.
    I dreamed last night of the three Weird Sisters.
    For you, their first prediction has come true.

MACBETH: I do not think about them.
    Yet, when we have an extra hour,
    We should meet and talk about what happened,
    If you would grant the time.

BANQUO: Whenever you would like, sir.

MACBETH: If you are loyal to me when the time comes,
    Honors shall come your way.

BANQUO: I will not lose any of my honor
    In seeking to add more to it.
    If I can be loyal and honorable at the same time,
    Then of course, I shall do so.

MACBETH: Sleep well, then!

BANQUO: Thank you, sir; the same to you.

(BANQUO *and* FLEANCE *exit.*)

MACBETH (*to his* SERVANT): Go tell my wife
    To ring the bell when my drink is ready.
    Then go on to bed.

(SERVANT *exits.*)

    Is this a dagger which I see before me,
    The handle toward my hand?
    Come, let me clutch you.
    I cannot touch you, and yet I still see you.
    Are you not, fatal vision, able to be felt
    As well as to be seen? Or are you only
    A dagger of the mind, a false creation
    Of my own fevered brain?
    I can see you still, in a form as real

As this one which I now draw.

(*He draws out his own, real dagger.*)

You show me the way that I was going,
And are the instrument I was going to use.
My eyes are either made fools by my other senses,
Or else they are better than the rest.
I can still see you,
And on your blade I see bits of blood,
That were not there before. There's no such thing.
This bloody business is making me see things.
Now, over half of the world, nature seems dead.
Wicked dreams come to those who sleep.
Sure and firm earth, hear not my steps.
Do not notice which way they walk.
I fear that the very stones tell where I am.
While I talk, Duncan still lives.
Words cool off the heat of the moment.

(*A bell rings.*)

Ah, the bell! My wife's signal
That the time has come.
I go, and it is done.
Hear it not, Duncan, for it is the sound
That calls you to your grave in the cold ground.

(MACBETH *exits.*)

Scene 2

The hall of the castle. LADY MACBETH *enters.*

LADY MACBETH: That which made them drunk
   Has made me bold.
   What has quenched their thirst

Has given me fire.
Listen! What's that noise?
It was the owl that shrieked,
The fatal bellman[1]
Which gives the sternest good-night.
The doors are open, and the drunken guards
Mock their King with snores.
I have drugged their drinks,
So that death and nature do fight about them,
Over whether they live or die.

MACBETH (*from another room*): Who's there? What's
   going on?

LADY MACBETH (*to herself*): Alas,
   I am afraid they have awakened,
   And it is not done yet.
   The attempt, and not the deed, ruins us.
   I put their daggers out in plain sight.
   He could not miss them.
   If Duncan had not resembled my own father
   As he slept, I would have done it myself.

(MACBETH *enters.*)

   My husband?

MACBETH: I have done the deed.
   Did you not hear a noise?

LADY MACBETH: I heard the owl scream
   And the crickets cry.
   Did you not speak?

---

1. **bellman** a man who rang a bell to mark the hours of the
   night or to announce a death; the sternest good-night is the
   final good-night of death.

MACBETH: When?

LADY MACBETH: Now.

MACBETH: As I came down the stairs?

LADY MACBETH: Yes.

MACBETH: Listen!
Who sleeps in the second chamber?

LADY MACBETH: Donalbain.

MACBETH (*looking at his hands*): This is a sorry sight.

LADY MACBETH: A foolish thought, to say a sorry sight.

MACBETH: Someone laughed in his sleep,
And another one cried, "Murder!"
They woke each other up.
I stood and listened to them,
But they said their prayers,
And went back to sleep.

LADY MACBETH: There are two guests
Sleeping in the same room.

MACBETH: One cried, "God bless us!"
And the other said "Amen."
It seemed to me that they had seen me
With these hangman's hands.
Listening to their fear, I could not say "Amen"
When they said, "God bless us!"

LADY MACBETH: Do not think of it so deeply.

MACBETH: But why could I not say "Amen"?
I had most need of blessing,
And "Amen" stuck in my throat.

LADY MACBETH: These deeds must not be thought of
Like this. If we continue to think this way,
It will drive us mad.

MACBETH: I thought I heard a voice cry,
"Sleep no more!
Macbeth does murder sleep," the innocent sleep,
Sleep, the death of each day's care,
Medicine for hurt minds,
The greatest nourisher in life's feast—

LADY MACBETH: What do you mean?

MACBETH: Still it cried, "Sleep no more!"
To all the house;
"Glamis has murdered sleep,
And therefore Cawdor shall sleep no more;
Macbeth shall sleep no more!"

LADY MACBETH: Who was it that cried out?
Why, worthy Thane,
You are wasting your strength
To think such insane thoughts.
Go get some water,
And wash this filthy evidence from your hand.
Why did you bring these daggers with you?
They must lie there. Go, take them back,
And smear the sleepy guards with blood.

MACBETH: I can't go back there.
I am afraid to think about what I have done;
I dare not look at it again.

LADY MACBETH: Weakling!
Give me the daggers.
The sleeping and the dead
Are just pictures of each other;
Only a child would be afraid of them.
I'll paint the faces of the guards
With Duncan's blood,
To make them look guilty.

(LADY MACBETH *exits. A knocking is heard.*)

MACBETH: Where is that knocking coming from?
Why is it that every noise frightens me?
What hands are these?
Will all great Neptune's ocean[2] wash this blood
Clean from my hand?
No, instead all the blood on my hand
Would make the green seas red.

(LADY MACBETH *enters.*)

LADY MACBETH: My hands are the same color as yours,
But I am ashamed to have a heart so white.
(*The sound of knocking.*) I hear a knocking
At the south entry. Let's go to our room.
A little water clears us of this deed;
How easy it is then!
Your courage seems to have deserted you.
(*More knocking.*) Listen! More knocking.
Put on your nightclothes.
We should look as if we've been sleeping.
Don't be so lost in your thoughts.

MACBETH: It would be better to be lost in thought
Than have to look at what I have done.
(*More knocking.*) Wake Duncan with your knocking!
I wish that you could!

(BOTH *exit.*)

---

2. Neptune's ocean Neptune was the Roman god of the sea.

Scene 3

The courtyard of the castle. A PORTER *enters. Knocking is heard.*

PORTER: Here's a knocking indeed! If a man were the porter at the gate of hell, he'd have a high old time turning the key. (*Knocking.*) Knock, knock, knock! Who's there, in the name of Beelzebub?[3] Here's a farmer, who hanged himself because he feared a low price on his grain. Have enough handkerchiefs on you! You'll need them to wipe the sweat off yourself down here! (*Knocking.*) Knock, knock! Who's there, in the other devil's name? Ah, it looks like a liar, who could swear both sides of a story were true. I see you could not lie your way into heaven! Oh, come in, liar! (*Knocking.*) Knock, knock, knock! Who's there? I believe it's an English tailor who has come this way for overcharging his customers. Come in, tailor; here it's hot enough for you to roast your goose.[4] (*Knocking.*) Knock, knock; it's never quiet! Who are you? But this place is too cold to be hell. I'll pretend to be the devil's porter no longer! (*Knocking.*) Coming! Coming! Don't forget to tip the porter!

(*The* PORTER *opens the gate.* MACDUFF *and* LENNOX *enter.*)

MACDUFF: Was it so late when you went to bed, friend? Is that why it took you so long to answer our knocking?

PORTER: It's true, sir. We were up drinking until three in the morning. As you know, sir, too much drink makes

---

3. **Beelzebub** the devil
4. **goose** a tailor's smoothing iron, named for its gooseneck handle

a person sleepy.

MACDUFF: Well, it certainly seems to have made you sleepy tonight.

PORTER: That it did, sir.

MACDUFF: Is your master awake?

(MACBETH *enters.*)

Oh, I see that our knocking has awakened him. Here he comes.

LENNOX: Good morning, noble sir.

MACBETH: Good morning, both of you.

MACDUFF: Is King Duncan awake, worthy Thane?

MACBETH: Not yet.

MACDUFF: He told me to wake him up early. I have almost missed the time he asked for.

MACBETH: I'll bring you to him.

MACDUFF: I know this is a joyful trouble to you, But it is still a bother.

MACBETH: The labor we enjoy cures our pain. This is the door.

MACDUFF: I'll be so bold as to go in and wake him. That's what he wants me to do.

(MACDUFF *exits.*)

LENNOX: Does the King plan to leave here today?

MACBETH: Yes, he does. At least, he did say so.

LENNOX: The night has been wild. Where we were sleeping, Our chimneys were blown down. And they say that there were strange cries

Heard in the air, strange screams of death,
And terrible predictions of fire and destruction
Coming in the near future. The owl,
That strange bird, shrieked all night long.
Some say the earth was feverish and shook.

MACBETH: It was a rough night.

LENNOX: I cannot remember any night
That was anything like it.

(MACDUFF *enters.*)

MACDUFF: Oh, horror, horror, horror!
Neither tongue nor heart can name or imagine it!

MACBETH *and* LENNOX (*together*): What's the matter?

MACDUFF: Destruction has now made its masterpiece!
A most unholy murder has broken open
The Lord's holy temple and has stolen
The life of the building!

MACBETH: What are you saying? The life?

LENNOX: Do you mean his Majesty?

MACDUFF: Approach his room,
And destroy your sight
With a new Gorgon.[5]
Do not ask me to speak.
See, and then speak yourselves.

(MACBETH *and* LENNOX *exit.*)

Awake, awake!
Ring the alarm bell! Murder and treason!

---

5. Gorgon In Greek mythology, one of three sisters who had
snakes for hair; the sight of a Gorgon turned the beholder to
stone.

Banquo and Donalbain! Malcolm! Awake!
Shake off this gentle sleep, which copies death,
And look on death itself!
Get up, get up, and see what has happened.
Malcolm! Banquo!
Rise up, as if from your graves.
Walk like spirits to see this horror!
Ring the bell!

(*A bell rings.* LADY MACBETH *enters.*)

LADY MACBETH: What is happening out here?
Why is such a terrible noise being made
To wake up the sleepers in the house?
Speak! Speak!

MACDUFF: Oh, gentle lady,
It is not for you to hear what I can speak.
To speak this in a woman's ear
Would murder her
As soon as the words were spoken.

(BANQUO *enters.*)

Oh, Banquo, Banquo,
Our royal master has been murdered!

LADY MACBETH: Woe, alas!
What, in our house?

BANQUO: It would be too cruel anywhere.
Dear Macduff, I beg you, take back what you said,
And say it is not so.

(MACBETH, LENNOX, *and* ROSS *enter.*)

MACBETH: If I had only died an hour ago,
I would have lived a good life.
From this moment on,

There is nothing serious in life.
All is but toys; honor and grace are dead;
The wine of life has been poured;
Only the dregs[6] are left.

(MALCOLM *and* DONALBAIN *enter.*)

DONALBAIN: What is wrong?

MACBETH: You are wrong, and you do not know it.
The spring, the head, the fountain of your blood
Is stopped. The very source of it is stopped.

DONALBAIN: What do you mean?

MACDUFF: Your royal father has been murdered.

MALCOLM: Oh, no! Who killed him?

LENNOX: It seems that his own guards did it.
Their hands and faces were all marked with blood,
And so were their daggers, which we found,
Unwiped, on their pillows.
No man's life was to be trusted with them.

MACBETH: Even so, I am sorry for the fury
That made me kill them.

MACDUFF: Why did you do that?

MACBETH: Who can be wise, confused,
Calm, and furious,
Loyal and neutral, all at once? No man.
The strength of my love for Duncan
Pushed me to action. Here lay Duncan,
His silver skin covered with his golden blood,
And there lay the murderers,
Covered in Duncan's blood, their daggers

---

6. dregs the solid bits of matter that settle to the bottom of a
liquid; the least desirable part

Right beside them.
Who could have held back from killing them?
Anyone would have done the same—
Anyone who had a heart to love
And in that heart enough courage
To make that love known.

LADY MACBETH (*fainting*): Help me!

MACDUFF: Look after the lady.

MALCOLM (*aside to* DONALBAIN): Why do we
    Hold our tongues, while everyone else
    Discusses this subject of such importance to us?

DONALBAIN (*aside to* MALCOLM): What can we say?
    Our fate might be hiding in some secret place,
    Ready to rush out and seize us.
    It's very possible that we are in danger.
    Let's go away from here.
    We can cry over our father's death later.

BANQUO (*seeing that* LADY MACBETH *has fainted*):
    Look after the lady.

(LADY MACBETH *is carried out.*)

Let's all go and get dressed,
And we'll meet back here later.
Then we can talk about
This most bloody piece of work,
And try to learn more about it.
Fears and doubts shake us.
In the great hand of God I stand,
And from there I shall fight
Against the unknown forces
Of treason and evil.

MACDUFF: And so do I.

ALL: So do all of us.

MACBETH: Let's put on our armor,
　　And meet in the hall together.

ALL: Good idea.

(ALL *but* MALCOLM *and* DONALBAIN *exit.*)

MALCOLM: What will you do?
　　Let's not have anything to do with them;
　　To show an unfelt sorrow is something
　　That false men do easily.
　　I'll go to England.

DONALBAIN: And I'll go to Ireland.
　　We'll probably be safer if we are apart.
　　Where we are,
　　There are daggers in men's smiles.
　　The nearer we're related to someone,
　　The closer we are to their danger.

MALCOLM: This murderous arrow
　　That has been shot
　　Has not yet landed.
　　It's probably still aiming for us.
　　Our safest way is to avoid the aim.
　　Let us not say good-bye to anyone.
　　We should just steal away.
　　There's honor in such a theft,
　　When, for all we know, no mercy's left.

Scene 4

Outside Macbeth's castle. ROSS *and an* OLD MAN *enter.*

OLD MAN: Threescore and ten[7] I can remember well;

---

7. threescore and ten　70 years

Within those years I have seen dreadful times
And strange things. But this sore night
Is the worst one I have ever experienced.

ROSS: Ah, good father,
You see that even the heavens seem troubled
By what has happened here tonight.
The clock tells us it is day,
And yet dark night seems to strangle the sun.[8]
Is it because night has triumphed
In this deed of darkness,
Or is day ashamed to look at it?
How can we explain the darkness
That covers the face of the earth
When living light should kiss it?

OLD MAN: It is unnatural,
Just like the deed that has been done.
Last Tuesday, a falcon,
Circling upward to the highest point
In her flight,
Was killed by a mousing owl.

ROSS: And Duncan's horses—
And this is surely very strange—
Beautiful and swift, the best of their breed,
Turned wild in nature.
They broke their stalls, and ran out,
Refusing to obey orders to stop.
They seemed to want to make
War with mankind.

OLD MAN: I heard that the horses
Ate each other.

---

8. dark night seems to strangle the sun Ross is describing
an eclipse.

ROSS: They did, to my amazement.
I saw it with my own eyes.

(MACDUFF *enters.*)

Here comes the good Macduff.
How's everything going, sir?

MACDUFF: Why, can't you see?

ROSS: Is it known who did this
More than bloody deed?

MACDUFF: Those guards that Macbeth killed.

ROSS: I can hardly believe it!
What good could they have hoped to accomplish?

MACDUFF: They were bribed by someone to do it.
Malcolm and Donalbain, the King's two sons,
Have stolen away and fled.
This puts upon them
Suspicion of the deed.

ROSS: Such an act would be completely
Against nature!
Why would they want to destroy
He who was responsible for their very life?
Now it is most likely that
The crown will pass to Macbeth.

MACDUFF: He has already been named King,
And has gone to Scone[9] to be crowned.

ROSS: Where is Duncan's body?

MACDUFF: It's been carried to Colmekill,
The sacred burial ground of Scottish kings.

ROSS: Will you go to Scone?

---

9. Scone   an ancient royal city of Scotland

36

MACDUFF: No, cousin. I'll go home, to Fife.

ROSS: Well, I'll go to Scone.

MACDUFF: Well, may you see things well done there.
Farewell!

ROSS: Farewell, father.

OLD MAN: God's blessings go with you,
And with those
Who would make good out of bad,
And friends out of foes!

(ALL *exit.*)

Act 3

Scene 1

Forres. The palace. BANQUO *enters.*

BANQUO: You have it now: King, Cawdor, Glamis, all,
Just as the Weird Sisters promised.
But I fear that you played most foully for it.
Yet it was said your sons shall not be kings,
But that I myself would be the root and father
Of many kings. If they were telling the truth—
As so far they seem to have been, about you—
May they not have told the truth about me as well?
If so, my hopes are strong! But hush, no more.

(*Trumpets sound.* MACBETH *enters, as King, followed by*
LADY MACBETH, LENNOX, ROSS, LORDS, *and* ATTENDANTS.)

MACBETH (*referring to* BANQUO): Here's our chief guest.

LADY MACBETH: If he had been forgotten,
It would have been like a gap in our great feast,
And would have ruined everything.

MACBETH: Tonight we are having a banquet, sir,
And I'd like you to be there.

BANQUO: As you wish, your Highness.

MACBETH: Are you going riding this afternoon?

BANQUO: Yes, my good lord.

MACBETH: Will you be riding far?

BANQUO: As far, my lord, as will fill up the time
Between now and supper.
Unless my horse goes too quickly,

I should be back about an hour after dark.

MACBETH: Do not fail to come to the feast.

BANQUO: My lord, I will not.

MACBETH: We hear our bloody cousins,
Malcolm and Donalbain, have taken refuge
In England and in Ireland. They have not confessed
To the cruel murder of their father.
Instead, they make up strange stories about it.
But we'll talk about that tomorrow.
Farewell, until you return this evening.
Is Fleance going with you?

BANQUO: Yes, my good lord. It's time we were going.

MACBETH: I hope your horses are swift
And sure of foot. Farewell.

(BANQUO *exits.* MACBETH *then speaks to the others.*)

Your time is free
Until seven o'clock tonight. To make company
Seem even sweeter then, we will stay alone
Until supper time. Until then, God be with you.

(ALL *but* MACBETH *and a* SERVANT *exit.* MACBETH *speaks to the* SERVANT.)

A word with you. We sent for some men.
Are they here yet?

SERVANT: They are, my lord.
They are outside the palace gate.

MACBETH: Bring them in.

(SERVANT *exits.*)

To be a king is nothing,
Unless one's position is safe.

Our fears about Banquo stick deep.
In his royalty of nature, there is much to be feared.
He is quite daring, and yet
He has a wisdom that guides his courage
To act in safety. He is the only one I fear.
Under him, my greatness is threatened.
He spoke to the three Weird Sisters
When they first put the name of king on me.
He made them speak to him. Then, like prophets,
They called him the father to a line of kings.
Upon my head they placed a fruitless crown,
And put a barren scepter[1] in my hands.
That scepter will be taken from my hands
By someone who is not a son of mine.
If the prophecies are correct,
I have committed all my crimes for Banquo's sons.
For them have I murdered the gracious Duncan,
And destroyed my own peace of mind.
I have given my soul to Satan, the enemy of all men,
Just to make Banquo's sons kings!
Rather than have this come true,
Let fate come into the battle, and fight on my side.

(*He hears a noise.*)

Who's there?

(*Macbeth's* SERVANT *enters, along with two* MURDERERS.)

Now go to the door,
And stay there until we call.

(SERVANT *exits.*)

---

1. **scepter**   the rod or staff carried by a ruler as a symbol of
royal power or authority

Was it not yesterday that we spoke together?

MURDERER 1: It was, your Highness.

MACBETH: Well, then,
Have you thought about what I said?
Do you understand that it was Banquo
Who was responsible for your bad fortune
In the past, and not my innocent self,
As you used to think?
I told you all this at our last meeting,
And I proved it clearly. I told you how you
Were led on by false promises
And then betrayed by Banquo.

MURDERER 1: You made it known to us.

MACBETH: I did so, and I went even further.
That is now the point of our second meeting.
Are you so patient and understanding
That you can let this go?
Do you plan to pray for this man and for his sons,
The same man whose heavy hand has ruined you
And made beggars of your sons forever?

MURDERER 2: We are men, my lord.

MACBETH: Yes, in the list of species,
You are described as men,
Just as hounds and greyhounds, mongrels,
Spaniels, curs, waterdogs, and wolves, are all
Called by the name of dogs.
The best kind of list shows the difference between
The swift, the slow, the wild,
The watchdog, and the hunter.
Each one is listed according to the
Particular gift that separates it from the rest.
The same is true of men.

Now, if you have a place in the list
Other than the worst rank, say so,
And I will give you this special assignment
Which will get rid of your enemy
And bring you closer to my heart and love.
For I wear my health sickly as long as he lives,
But in his death, my life will be perfect.

MURDERER 2: My lord, I am one who is so angry
At the evil blows given me by the world,
That I am reckless about
What I do to spite the world.

MURDERER 1: And I am another,
So weary with disasters, pulled by bad luck,
That I would bet my life on any chance,
To make it better, or be rid of it.

MACBETH: You know that Banquo was your enemy.

BOTH MURDERERS: True, my lord.

MACBETH: He is my enemy, too, and I hate him so much,
That every minute of his being feels like
A knife thrust to my heart.
I know that I could, with all my power,
Sweep him from my sight and be rid of him,
Yet I must not do that.
Certain friends that are both his and mine
Would be very angry if I did.
That is why I must ask your help.
Take care of this business,
But do not let any suspicion fall on me.

MURDERER 2: My lord, we shall do as you command.

MACBETH: Your spirits shine through you.
Within the hour, I will tell you
Where to plant yourselves.

I will tell you the exact time he will be there,
To the very moment. It must be done tonight,
And it must be done away from the palace.
Always remember that I am not to be suspected.
Do not make any mistakes.
Fleance, his son, will be with him.
His death is no less important to me
Than his father's. He must also face the fate
Of that dark hour. Now, go wait outside.
I'll come to you soon.

BOTH MURDERERS: We shall wait outside, my lord.

MACBETH: I'll speak to you soon.

(MURDERERS *exit.* MACBETH *speaks to himself.*)

It is arranged. Banquo, your soul's flight,
If it goes to heaven, must go tonight.

(MACBETH *exits.*)

Scene 2

The palace. LADY MACBETH *and a* SERVANT *enter.*

LADY MACBETH: Is Banquo gone from court?

SERVANT: Yes, madam, but he returns again tonight.

LADY MACBETH: Tell the King I would like to see him
For a few words.

SERVANT: Madam, I will.

(SERVANT *exits.*)

LADY MACBETH: Nothing is ours, all is spent,
When we have our desires, but are not content.
It is safer to be that which we destroy
Than to live by destruction in doubtful joy.

(MACBETH *enters.*)

My lord! Why do you stay alone,
With only sad thoughts as companions?
You are entertaining those thoughts
That should have died
With them you are thinking about.
Things that cannot be changed
Should not be thought of. What's done is done.

MACBETH: We have cut the snake, not killed it;
Soon she'll close and be herself,[2]
And we will be in great danger.
Let the whole universe get out of joint,
And let both heaven and earth suffer,
Rather than have us eat our meals in fear,
And sleep with those terrible dreams
That shake us nightly.
It would be better to be with the dead,
Whom we, to gain our peace, have sent to peace,
Than to suffer this constant torture in our minds.
Duncan is in his grave;
After life's fitful fever he sleeps well.
Nothing can touch him further.

LADY MACBETH: Come on,
My gentle lord, smooth over your rugged looks;
Be bright and happy among your guests tonight.

MACBETH: So shall I, love; and so, I hope, shall you.
Let your attention be given to Banquo;
Show him special favor, both with your eyes
And with your words.

---

2. close and be herself This refers to a folk belief that a snake, cut in two, can later join its parts together.

For the time being, we are unsafe, so we must
Bathe our guests in these flattering streams,
And make our faces masks for our hearts,
Disguising what they are.

LADY MACBETH: You must stop this.

MACBETH: Oh, full of scorpions is my mind, dear wife!
You know that Banquo and his Fleance live.

LADY MACBETH: But they won't live forever.

MACBETH: There's comfort in that, so be joyful.
Before the bat flies out of its cave
Into the darkness of the night,
There shall be done
A dreadful deed.

LADY MACBETH: What's to be done?

MACBETH: Be innocent of the knowledge, dearest,
Until you can applaud the deed. Come, dark night,
Blindfold the tender eye of pitiful day,
And with your bloody and invisible hand
Cancel and tear to pieces that great bond[3]
That keeps me pale! Light thickens,
And the crow flies to the woods;
Good things of day begin to droop and drowse,
While night's black agents to their preys do go.
You wonder at my words, but hold still;
Evil things gain strength through evil.
So, please, go with me.

(BOTH *exit.*)

---

3. that great bond refers to both Banquo's life and to the
promise made by the Witches to Banquo

Scene 3

A park near the palace. Three MURDERERS *enter.*

MURDERER 1: Who told you to join us?

MURDERER 3: Macbeth.

MURDERER 2 (*to* MURDERER 1): We have no reason
    To mistrust him. He has come to deliver our orders
    And to tell us exactly what to do.

MURDERER 1: Then stand with us;
    The west still glimmers with some streaks of day.
    The late traveler is hurrying along
    To get to an inn before dark.
    Those whom we are waiting for
    Should be coming along soon.

MURDERER 3: Listen! I hear horses.

BANQUO (*offstage*): Give us a light there!

MURDERER 2: That must be Banquo.
    The rest of those on the guest list
    Are already in the banquet hall.

MURDERER 1: The groom is taking the horses
    To the stable. Banquo and Fleance
    Will be walking the rest of the way
    From the palace gate to the castle.

MURDERER 3: They'll be walking right by us.

(BANQUO *and* FLEANCE *enter.* FLEANCE *carries a torch.*)

MURDERER 2: I see a light! They're almost here!

MURDERER 3: Get ready!

BANQUO: It looks like rain tonight.

MURDERER 1: Let it come down!

(MURDERER 1 *strikes out the light, while the others attack* BANQUO.)

BANQUO: Oh, treachery! Run, good Fleance,
Run, run, run!
Avenge me later! Farewell!

(BANQUO *dies*. FLEANCE *escapes.*)

MURDERER 3: Who struck out the light?

MURDERER 1: Wasn't that the way to do it?

MURDERER 3: There's only one down; the son has fled.

MURDERER 2: We have failed in the
Most important part of the job.

MURDERER 1: Well, let's go
And tell Macbeth how much is done.

(ALL *exit.*)

Scene 4

A hall in the palace. A banquet is prepared. MACBETH,
LADY MACBETH, ROSS, LENNOX, LORDS, *and* ATTENDANTS
enter.

MACBETH: You know your own ranks.
Take your proper places at the table.
To one and all, a hearty welcome.

LORDS: Thanks to your Majesty.

MACBETH: We will mingle with our guests
And play the humble host.
Our hostess will remain seated, but soon
We shall request her words of welcome.

LADY MACBETH: Say it for me, sir, to all our friends,
For my heart says they are welcome.

(MURDERER 1 *enters and stands at the door.*)

MACBETH (*to* LADY MACBETH): See, they meet you
　With their hearts' thanks.
　Both sides of the table are even;
　I'll sit here in the middle, in a few minutes.
　Enjoy yourselves, everyone.
　Soon we'll have a toast to start off the meal.

(MACBETH *walks toward the door as the banquet guests
talk among themselves. He speaks to* MURDERER 1.)

　There's blood on your face.

MURDERER 1: It is Banquo's.

MACBETH: It's better outside you than inside him.
　Is he dead?

MURDERER 1: My lord, his throat is cut.
　That I did for him.

MACBETH: You are the best of the cut-throats,
　But he is also good who did the same for Fleance.
　If you did it, you are surely the best.

MURDERER 1: Most royal sir,
　Fleance escaped.

MACBETH: Oh, no! This is terrible.
　My life would have been perfect,
　Whole as the marble, firm as the rock,
　But now I am confined, hemmed in[4]
　By doubts and fears. But Banquo's dead?

MURDERER 1: Yes, my lord. Dead in a ditch he lies,
　With twenty gashes in his head,
　The least of which would have killed him.

---

4. hemmed in　surrounded

MACBETH: Thanks for that.
　　The grown serpent lies dead;
　　The worm that has escaped will soon have venom,
　　But he has no teeth yet.
　　Leave now. We'll talk again tomorrow.

(MURDERER 1 *exits.*)

LADY MACBETH: My royal lord,
　　We have guests. A feast is no fun
　　When the host fails to make the guests feel welcome.
　　Mere feeding of oneself is best done at home;
　　Away from home, ceremony is the sauce to the meat.
　　A meal away from home is bare without it.
　　So act like a proper host, and
　　Pay attention to your guests.

(*The* GHOST OF BANQUO, *which is visible only to*
MACBETH, *enters.* MACBETH *does not see it yet. The* GHOST
sits in MACBETH'S *place.*)

MACBETH: Dear wife! Thank you for reminding me.
　　Now, here's to a good meal, good appetites,
　　And good health to all!

LENNOX: May it please your Highness to sit.

MACBETH: Here we would have all our country's
　　Noblemen seated under one roof,
　　If only the gracious Banquo were present.
　　I hope that his reason for not being here
　　Has something to do with unkindness
　　Rather than some terrible accident.

ROSS: His absence sir,
　　Breaks his promise. Would it please your Highness
　　To grace us with your royal company?

MACBETH: The table is full.

LENNOX: Here is an empty seat, sir.

MACBETH: Where?

LENNOX: Here, my good lord.

(LENNOX *notices that* MACBETH *seems shocked at something.* MACBETH *has just seen* BANQUO'S GHOST.)

　　What's wrong, sir?

MACBETH: Which of you have done this?

LORDS: What, my good lord?

MACBETH (*to the* GHOST): You cannot say I did it!
　　Never shake your bloody head at me.

ROSS: Gentlemen, rise; his Highness is not well.

LADY MACBETH: Sit, worthy friends;
　　My lord is often like this,
　　And has been since his youth.
　　Please, stay seated.
　　The fit is temporary; in a moment
　　He will again be well. If you make a scene,
　　You shall offend him and make it worse.
　　Eat, and pay no attention to him.
　　(*aside, to* MACBETH) Are you a man?

MACBETH: Yes, and a bold one, who dares look at that,
　　Which might even frighten the devil.

LADY MACBETH (*aside to* MACBETH): Nonsense!
　　You are acting just as you did before the murder.
　　This is the dagger in the air that you said you saw—
　　The one that led you to Duncan.
　　These weaknesses and outbursts
　　Belong in a woman's story told by a fireside,
　　On the authority of her grandma. Shame itself!

Why do you make such faces?
You're looking only at a stool.

MACBETH: No, see there! Behold! Look!
Can't you see it? Why, what do I care?
I see it, and that's enough!
If our graves can send
Those that we bury back to haunt us,
Then perhaps we should let birds eat the dead.
That way, the ghosts could not rise.

(GHOST *vanishes.*)

LADY MACBETH (*aside to* MACBETH):
What is wrong with you?
Have you completely lost your mind?

MACBETH: As I am standing here, I saw him.

LADY MACBETH (*aside to* MACBETH): Shame on you!

MACBETH: Blood has been shed before this,
In the olden times,
Before human laws made the nation gentle.
Yes, and since then, too, murders have been done
That were too terrible to hear about.
In the past, when the brains were out,
The man would die, and that was the end of it.
But now the dead rise again,
With twenty mortal gashes on their heads,
And push us from our stools.
This is stranger than such a murder is.

LADY MACBETH: My worthy lord,
Your noble friends are waiting for you.

MACBETH: I almost forgot.
Do not wonder at me, my most worthy friends.
I have a strange illness, which is nothing

To those who know me. Come, love and health to all,
Then I'll sit down. Give me some wine, a full glass;
I drink to the general joy of the whole table,
And to our dear friend Banquo, whom we miss.
I wish that he were here! To all and to him we drink,
And all to all.

LORDS: Hear, hear!

(GHOST *enters again.*)

MACBETH (*to the* GHOST):
Quit my sight! Let the earth hide you!
Your bones have no marrow; your blood is cold;
You cannot see from those eyes
That you glare at me with!

LADY MACBETH: Think of this, good lords,
As just a thing of custom. It's nothing more,
Only it spoils the pleasure of the time.

MACBETH (*to the* GHOST): What a man dares, I dare.
Approach me like a rugged Russian bear,
An armed rhinoceros, or a tiger;
Take any shape but that, and my firm nerves
Shall never tremble. Or be alive again,
And dare me to a fight to the death with your sword.
If I tremble at all, call me a little girl's doll.
Go away, horrible shadow!
Unreal mockery, go away!

(GHOST *vanishes.*)

Why, now it is gone.
I am myself again. Please, be seated, all.

LADY MACBETH: You have ruined the banquet,
And spoiled the whole evening

With your amazing behavior.

MACBETH: Can such things appear,
And sweep over us like a summer cloud,
Without our special wonder? You make me
A stranger to myself
When I think you can see such sights,
And keep the natural ruby of your cheeks,
When mine are white with fear.

ROSS: What sights, my lord?

LADY MACBETH: I pray you, do not speak to him.
He grows worse and worse.
Questions enrage him. At once, good night.
Stand not upon the order of your going,[5]
But go at once.

LENNOX: Good night. May better health
Come to his Majesty!

LADY MACBETH: A kind good night to all!

(LORDS *exit.*)

MACBETH: It wants revenge, I know.
Blood will be paid back in blood.
Stones have been known to move
And trees to speak.[6]
What time is it?

LADY MACBETH: It is almost midnight.

---

5. **Stand not upon the order of your going** Lady Macbeth is asking her guests to leave quickly and not take time to leave in the order of their ranks, as was the custom.
6. **Stones have been known to move, and trees to speak** This refers to two superstitions: that stones refuse to stay over the grave of a man who has been murdered, and that a tree revealed a murder in the *Aeneid,* a Roman story.

MACBETH: What do you think of the fact that
Macduff refused to come to the coronation
And did not come to this banquet, either?

LADY MACBETH: Did he send a messenger, sir?

MACBETH: No, he didn't,
But I will send one to him tomorrow.
I have at least one spy among the servants
In every nobleman's house, so I know
What Macduff has been saying.
Tomorrow I will visit the Weird Sisters again.
They shall tell me more about the future.
For now, I am determined to know,
By the worst methods, the worst.
For my own good, all other matters
Must come second.
I am standing so deep in blood now,
That if it were a river, I would have to cross it.
It is easier to go to the other side
Than to wade back at this point.
I have strange ideas in my head,
Which must be acted upon.

LADY MACBETH: You need some sleep.

MACBETH: Come, we'll go to sleep.
My strange vision of the Ghost
Was from the fear of a beginner in evil.
We are yet but young in such things.

(BOTH *exit.*)

Scene 5

Forres. LENNOX *and another* LORD *enter.*

LENNOX: It seems strange to me how everyone

Who has been close to Macbeth has suffered.
Remember the gracious Duncan and
What happened to him.
And the brave Banquo, out walking late,
Killed by his own son Fleance,
Or so Macbeth would have us believe.
After all, Fleance fled; men must not walk too late.
And who cannot help thinking how monstrous
It was for Malcolm and Donalbain
To kill their gracious father! A terrible thing!
How it did grieve Macbeth! Did he not immediately
Kill the two guards in an angry rage?
Anyone could see that those two guards
Had been drinking too much and were sound asleep.
Wasn't that a noble act on Macbeth's part?
Yes, and it was a wise act, too,
For it would have angered any heart alive
To hear the guards deny their deed.
I wonder what Macbeth would do if he had
Duncan's sons and Fleance under lock and key.
I'm sure they'd find out the punishment
For killing a father. But, enough about that!
I hear that Macduff lives in disgrace, too,
Because he didn't come to the tyrant's feast.
Macbeth must think we are all fools
Who can't see what has been happening.
Sir, can you tell me where Macduff is now?

LORD: Malcolm, Duncan's son
(From whom this tyrant Macbeth took the crown),
Is in England now, at King Edward's court.
Macduff has gone to England, too,
To help Malcolm persuade the English king
To assemble an army against Macbeth,

Who has been preparing for war against England.
Macbeth has asked Macduff for help in this war,
And was refused.
If Malcolm and Macduff are successful, we may again
    someday
Live in peace, without fear of bloody knives at
    banquets.

LENNOX: I hope that some holy angel
Flies to the court of England to help Macduff.
May a swift blessing return to our suffering country!

LORD: I'll send my prayers with him.

(BOTH *exit.*)

Act 4

Scene 1

A cavern. In the middle, a boiling cauldron. Thunder. The three WITCHES *enter.*

WITCH 1: Round about the cauldron go;
　　　Into the pot these things we'll throw:
　　　Poison toad that's been under cold stone
　　　For days that number thirty-one,
　　　From its sweat we have venom got—
　　　This goes first in the charmed pot.

ALL: Double, double, toil and trouble;
　　　Fire burn and cauldron bubble.

WITCH 2: From the swamp I got this snake,
　　　In the cauldron boil and bake;
　　　Eye of newt and toe of frog,
　　　Wool of bat and tongue of dog,
　　　Adder's tongue and blind-worm's sting,
　　　Lizard's leg and owl's wing,
　　　For a charm of powerful trouble,
　　　Evil broth, boil and bubble.

ALL: Double, double, toil and trouble;
　　　Fire burn and cauldron bubble.

WITCH 3: Tooth of wolf, and dragon's scale,
　　　Witches' mummy, eye and nail,
　　　Parts of hungry salt-sea shark,
　　　Root of hemlock dug in the dark,
　　　Add a little, then a lot,
　　　All these go into the pot.

ALL: Double, double, toil and trouble;

Fire burn and cauldron bubble.

WITCH 2: By the tingling in my thumbs,
Something wicked this way comes.
Open, locks,
Whoever knocks!

(MACBETH *enters.*)

MACBETH: You secret, midnight hags!
What are you doing?

ALL: A deed without a name.

MACBETH: I have come to ask you some questions.

WITCH 1: Speak.

WITCH 2: Demand.

WITCH 3: We'll answer.

WITCH 1: Would you rather hear it from our mouths,
Or from our masters' mouths?

MACBETH: Call them. Let me see them.

WITCH 1: Pour in the blood of a pig
That has eaten her litter.
Add some sweat taken from a murderer's gallows.
Throw these things into the flame.

(*Thunder.* FIRST VISION, *a Head wearing armor, appears,
rising out of the cauldron.*)

MACBETH: Tell me, unknown power—

WITCH 1: He knows what you are thinking.
Listen to his speech, but say nothing.

VISION 1: Macbeth! Macbeth! Macbeth! Beware Macduff;
Beware the Thane of Fife. I go. I've said enough.

(VISION 1 *disappears into the cauldron.*)

MACBETH: Whatever you are, for your warning, thanks;
   You have touched on the same fears I already have.
   But one word more—

WITCH 1: He will not appear again.
   Here's another,
   More powerful than the first.

(*Thunder.* SECOND VISION, *a Bloody Child, appears, rising out of the cauldron.*)

VISION 2: Macbeth! Macbeth! Macbeth!

MACBETH: If I had three ears, I'd hear you.

VISION 2: Be strong, bold, and firm; laugh to scorn
   The power of man; for none of woman born
   Shall harm Macbeth.

(VISION 2 *disappears into the cauldron.*)

MACBETH: Then live, Macduff!
   I have no reason to fear you.
   But, on the other hand, I'll make doubly sure,
   And make a deal with fate: you shall not live!
   So I may put all my terrible fears
   To rest, and sleep in spite of thunder.

(*Thunder.* THIRD VISION, *a Child crowned, with a tree in his hand, appears, rising out of the cauldron.*)

   What is this
   That rises like the son of a king,
   And wears upon his baby-brow the crown
   And signs of royalty?

ALL: Listen, but do not speak to it.

VISION 3: Be as brave as a lion, and be proud.
   Do not worry about your enemies.

Macbeth shall never be conquered until
The Forest of Birnam comes to Dunsinane Hill
And fights against him.

(VISION 3 *disappears into the cauldron.*)

MACBETH: That will never be.
Who can force a forest into military service?
Who can tell the tree to move his earth-bound root?
Sweet words! Good!
Rebel armies will not rise until the wood
Of Birnam rises. Our high-placed Macbeth
Shall live a long life, as nature intended.
Yet my heart throbs to know one thing.
Tell me, if you know so much,
Shall Banquo's sons ever
Reign in this kingdom?

ALL: Seek to know no more.

MACBETH: I must know! Deny me this,
And an eternal curse fall on you! Let me know.

WITCH 1: Show!

WITCH 2: Show!

WITCH 3: Show!

ALL: Show his eyes, and grieve his heart;
Come like shadows, so depart!

(*A show of* EIGHT KINGS *and* BANQUO, *the last, with a
mirror in his hand, rises from the cauldron.*)

MACBETH (*speaking to each* KING *in turn*):
You are too much like the spirit of Banquo!
Go back down! Your face burns my eyeballs.
And your hair is golden, like the first one.
A third is like the others. Filthy hags!

Why do you show me this? A fourth!
Stop looking, eyes!
What, will the line stretch out to the crack of doom?
Another yet! A seventh! I'll see no more.
And yet the eighth appears, carrying a mirror
Which shows me many more. Some I see
Wear two crowns and carry three scepters.[1]
Horrible sight! They all resemble Banquo.
Now, I see, it is true. They will all be kings.
The blood-spattered Banquo smiles at me,
And points at them, as if to say they come from him.

(VISION 3 *vanishes, disappearing into the cauldron.*
MACBETH *then speaks to the* WITCHES.)

What, is this so?

WITCH 1: Yes, sir, all this is so. But why
Does Macbeth seem so amazed?
Come, sisters, let's take our leave.
I'll charm the air to give a sound,
While you perform your dances round;
So this great king may kindly say,
We answered his questions on this day.

(*Music. The* WITCHES *dance, and then they vanish.*)

MACBETH: Where are they? Gone? Let this evil hour
Stand as accursed in the calendar.
Come in, whoever is out there!

(LENNOX *enters.*)

---

1. **wear two crowns and carry three scepters** refers to the
fact that some of Banquo's descendants would be king of two or
three countries at once

LENNOX: What is your Grace's will?

MACBETH: Did you see the Weird Sisters?

LENNOX: No, my lord.

MACBETH: Didn't they pass by you?

LENNOX: No, indeed, my lord.

MACBETH: Even the air on which they ride is evil!
I heard the galloping of a horse;
Who was it that came by?

LENNOX: Two or three of us have come, my lord,
To bring you word that
Macduff has fled to England.

MACBETH: Fled to England!

LENNOX: Yes, my good lord.

MACBETH (*aside*): If I hadn't come to this cavern
I might have had the time to stop Macduff.
From this moment on,
As soon as I think about doing something,
I shall do it immediately. Even now,
To crown my thoughts with acts,
Be it thought and done:
I will surprise Macduff's castle:
I will give the edge of the sword
To his wife, his babies, and any unlucky relatives
Who might happen to be there at the time.
I will not boast about it like a fool;
I'll order this done before my anger cools.

(ALL *exit.*)

Scene 2

Fife. Macduff's castle. LADY MACDUFF, *her* SON, *and* ROSS *enter.*

LADY MACDUFF: What had he done, to make him
Flee Scotland and go to England?

ROSS: You must have patience, madam.

LADY MACDUFF: He had none;
His flight was madness. Leaving Scotland
Makes him look like a traitor.

ROSS: You do not know
If he left out of wisdom or fear.

LADY MACDUFF: Wisdom! To leave his wife,
To leave his babies, his castle, and his title,
In a place from which he himself does fly?
He loves us not. He lacks natural affection.
Even the poor wren, the smallest of birds,
Will fight against the owl to protect
The young ones in her nest.
He is all fear and no love.
He has no wisdom, when running away
Goes so much against reason.

ROSS: My dearest cousin, I beg you, calm down.
Your husband is noble, wise, and careful.
He knows the disorder of the time.
I dare not speak further;
But the times are cruel when we are accused
Of being traitors without knowing our treason;
When we believe every frightening rumor
Based only on what we fear might be true,
And float upon a wild and violent sea
Moving each way the waves take us.

I must leave you now.
It shall not be long before I am here again.
When things get to their worst, they will stop,
Or else climb back up to where they were before.
My pretty cousin, my blessings upon you!

LADY MACDUFF (*referring to her* SON):
He has a father, and yet he's fatherless.

ROSS: I am so much a fool, if I stay any longer,
I fear I would start crying.
That would only disgrace me
And make you uncomfortable.
I take my leave at once.

(ROSS *exits.*)

LADY MACDUFF: My son, your father's dead;
And what will you do now? How will you live?

SON: As birds do, Mother.

LADY MACDUFF: What, with worms and flies?

SON: No, with whatever I can get, as they do.

LADY MACDUFF: Poor bird. You would never fear
The net or the traps, the hunters or the snares.

SON: Why should I, Mother? Poor birds are not hunted.
My father is not dead, no matter what you say.

LADY MACDUFF: Yes, he is dead.
What will you do for a father?

SON: No, what will you do for a husband?

LADY MACDUFF: Why, I can buy me twenty at any market.

SON: Then you'll buy them to sell again.

LADY MACDUFF: You speak with such wit!

SON: Was my father a traitor, Mother?

LADY MACDUFF: Yes, he was.

SON: What is a traitor?

LADY MACDUFF: Why, one who swears and lies.

SON: And do all traitors do so?

LADY MACDUFF: Every one that does so is a traitor,
And must be hanged.

SON: And must all who swear and lie be hanged?

LADY MACDUFF: Every one.

SON: Who must hang them?

LADY MACDUFF: Why, the honest men.

SON: Then the liars and swearers are fools; for there are
enough liars and swearers to beat the honest men
and hang them!

LADY MACDUFF: Now, God help you, poor monkey!
But what will you do for a father?

SON: If he were dead, you'd weep for him; if you don't
weep for him, it is a good sign that I will quickly
have a new father.

LADY MACDUFF: How you talk!

(A MESSENGER enters.)

MESSENGER: Bless you, fair lady! You don't know me,
Though I know who you are.
I fear that some danger is approaching you,
And it is close.
Even though I am a man without a title,
Please take my advice, and get away from here.
Leave immediately, with your little ones.
I am sorry to frighten you,
But to actually harm you would be far worse,

And there are those who do want to harm you.
Heaven help you! I dare stay here no longer.

(MESSENGER *exits.*)

LADY MACDUFF: Where should I go?
I have done no harm. But I remember now
That I am in this earthly world. To do harm
Is often praiseworthy. To do good, sometimes,
Is dangerous foolishness. Why then, alas,
Do I put up that womanly defense,
To say I have done no harm?

(MURDERERS *enter.*)

Who are you?

MURDERER 1: Where is your husband?

LADY MACDUFF: I hope he is in no place so bad
That people like you might find him.

MURDERER 1: He's a traitor.

SON: You lie, you filthy villain!

MURDERER 1 (*stabbing him*): What, you egg!
Young child of a traitor!

SON: He has killed me, Mother.
Run away, I pray you!

(SON *dies.* LADY MACDUFF *exits, crying "Murder!"*
MURDERERS *exit, following her.*)

Scene 3

England. Before the King's palace. MALCOLM *and*
MACDUFF *enter.*

MALCOLM: Let us seek out some lonely shade,

And there weep until we have no more tears.

MACDUFF: Let us instead
Pick up our swords, and like good men
March back to our downfallen land.
Each new morning,
New widows howl, new orphans cry,
New sorrows strike heaven on the face,
So that heaven echoes as if feeling Scotland's pain,
Yelling out its own cries of sorrow.

MALCOLM: I'll cry for what I know is happening,
I will change what I can, when the time is right.
What you have said may be true.
This tyrant, whose name alone blisters our tongues,
Was once thought honest; you have loved him well.
He has not touched you yet. That makes me think
You might still be working for him.
Perhaps you plan to win favor with Macbeth
By betraying me to him.
You might offer up a weak, poor, innocent lamb
To appease an angry god.

MACDUFF: I am not treacherous.

MALCOLM: But Macbeth is.
A good and virtuous nature might act dishonorably
Under a king's order. But I ask your pardon
For these thoughts. Whatever you are,
My thoughts cannot change you.
Angels are still bright, though the brightest[2] fell.
Even though evil tries to wear the face of grace,
True grace must still look the same.

MACDUFF: I have lost my hopes.

---

2. the brightest Lucifer, the fallen angel

MALCOLM: Even though I wonder why you left
Your wife and child, those strong knots of love,
Without saying good-bye to them,
I really have no reason to mistrust you.
You may be just and true, no matter what I think.

MACDUFF: Bleed, bleed, poor country!
Great tyranny! Farewell, my lord.
I would not be the villain that you suspect
For all the power that is in the tyrant's grasp,
And the rich East as well.

MALCOLM: Do not be offended by my words.
I do not mistrust you completely.
I think our country suffers greatly under Macbeth.
It weeps, it bleeds; and each new day a gash
Is added to her wounds. I think I could find
Much support for my cause.
In fact, the gracious King of England has offered
Many thousands to help me. But, for all this,
When I shall tread upon the tyrant's head,
Or wear it on my sword, still my poor country
Will have more troubles than it had before.
It may suffer more, and in more ways, than ever,
By him who wears the crown after Macbeth.

MACDUFF: Who would that be?

MALCOLM: It is myself I mean. I know my faults.
If I were on the throne, I would be even
More evil than Macbeth. The poor country
Would remember him as a lamb,
Compared to me.

MALCOLM: Nobody could be worse than Macbeth.

MALCOLM: I grant that he is brutal,
Lustful, greedy, false, deceitful,

Violent, evil, smacking of every sin
That has a name. But there is no bottom, none,
To my evil. Your wives, your daughters,
Your old women, and your maids, could never
Be safe from me. And if anyone tried to stop me,
He would be sorry. Better Macbeth
Than someone like me to reign.

MACDUFF: Such thoughts are not right.
They have been the cause of great unhappiness
And the fall of many kings. But do not be afraid
To take upon yourself that which is yours. You may
Enjoy the company of many willing women,
Who would be happy to dedicate themselves to you.

MALCOLM: That is not my only vice.
I am also so greedy that, if I were King,
I would take the nobles' lands,
Take this one's jewels and that one's house.
The more I would have, the more I would want.
Eventually, I would cause unfair quarrels
Against the good and loyal,
Destroying them so I could get their wealth.

MACDUFF: Such greed is even more dangerous
Than youthful lust, and it has been
The sword that killed many kings. Yet do not fear:
Scotland has plenty of riches to satisfy you
Without hurting anyone. All these vices
Can be endured, considering your good points.

MALCOLM: But I have none. The king-becoming graces—
Such as justice, honesty, discipline, stability,
Generosity, strength, mercy, humility,
Devotion, patience, courage, and strength—
I have no trace of them. Instead, I have a tendency

Toward crime, showing it in many ways.
No, if I had power, I would be dangerous.
I might cause the end of all peace on earth.

MACDUFF: Oh, Scotland, Scotland!

MALCOLM: If such a one as me is fit to be king, speak.
I am as I have said.

MACDUFF: Fit to govern!
No, not even to live. Oh, miserable nation,
With a blood-thirsty tyrant on the throne,
When will you see good days again, now that
The rightful wearer of your crown
Admits he is not fit to rule?
Malcolm, your royal father, Duncan,
Was a most sainted king; the queen who
Was your mother lived a life of daily prayer.
Farewell! These evils that you confess
Mean I can never return to Scotland. Oh, my country,
Your hope ends here!

MALCOLM: Macduff, your noble passion
For Scotland has cleared my mind of any doubts
I had concerning your loyalty. I was testing you,
And you proved to me that you are a man of
Truth and honor. The evil Macbeth has often tried
To win me into his power by offering me
Women, power, and riches, but you did not,
Even when I told you I wanted those things.
Let me assure you that those evils
Are strangers to me. I have never even
Been with a woman, I have never lied,
I have hardly even wanted what was my own.
At no time have I broken my faith,
And I would never betray anyone.

I am a good and decent man, who delights
In truth as much as in life. The first lie
I ever told was to tell you that I was evil.
What I am truly, is yours,
And my poor country's, to command.
All I want is to serve my country well.
In fact, before you got here,
An English general, with 10,000 warlike men,
Ready for battle, was setting forth to Scotland.
Now we'll go together! But why are you silent?

MACDUFF: First you tell me one thing, and
Then you say another.
Such welcome and unwelcome news all at once
Is hard to figure out.

(A DOCTOR *enters.*)

MALCOLM (*to* MACDUFF): Well, we'll talk more later.
(*to the* DOCTOR) Is King Edward coming?

DOCTOR: Yes, sir. A crowd of sick people
Waits outside for him. Each wants to be cured.
No doctor can do anything for them,
But at Edward's touch, they are cured.
He must have a gift from heaven.

MALCOLM: Thank you, Doctor.

(DOCTOR *exits.*)

MACDUFF: What disease is he talking about?

MALCOLM: It's called the evil, or the king's evil.[3]
It is most miraculous that this good king
Can help those who have the disease.

---

3. the king's evil   scrofula, a disease affecting the lymph nodes
of the neck

Often, since I have been here in England,
I have seen him do it. How he does it,
Only he knows. But very sick people,
All swollen and with big sores on their skin,
Come to him. They are pitiful to the eye,
And surgery cannot help them.
Edward cures them by hanging a golden coin
Around their necks and saying some prayers.
He must be a very holy man to be able to do this.

(ROSS *enters.*)

MACDUFF: See, who comes here?

MALCOLM: He is my countryman,
But I do not know him.

MACDUFF: My gentle cousin, welcome to England.

MALCOLM: Oh, now I know who he is!
I have been away from Scotland too long!
May all that keeps me from home soon change!

ROSS: Sir, I wish the same thing.

MACDUFF: Is Scotland still the same?

ROSS: Alas, poor country!
It is almost afraid to know itself.
It cannot be called our mother, but only our grave.
Only those who know nothing are ever seen smiling.
Sighs and groans and shrieks tear the air.
Violent sorrow seems a common emotion.
The bell for the dead rings so often
That no one asks anymore who has died.
Good men die before the flowers in their hats,
Before they have had time to get sick.

MACDUFF: Poor Scotland!

MALCOLM: What's the newest grief?

ROSS: Anyone who tells what happened an hour ago
Is hissed at. Hour-long news is already old.
Every minute it's something new.

MACDUFF: How is my wife?

ROSS: Why, well.[4]

MACDUFF: And all my children?

ROSS: Well, too.

MACDUFF: The tyrant has not battered at their peace?

ROSS: No, they were well at peace when I left them.

MACDUFF: Don't be so stingy with your words!
What's happening in Scotland?

ROSS: On my way here to bring you some sad news,
I heard a rumor that many worthy Scots
Had taken up arms to rebel against the tyrant.
I have reason to believe this rumor is true, for
I saw the tyrant's soldiers were out.
We truly need help now.
(*to* MALCOLM) If you were in Scotland,
Soldiers would follow you. Even women would fight
To overthrow the present rule.

MALCOLM: You can assure them that
We're on our way. The gracious King of England
Has lent us good Siward and 10,000 men;
An older and a better soldier cannot be found.

ROSS: I wish I could answer
Your good news with good news of my own!
But I have words that should be howled out

---

4. well at peace; Ross is using a double meaning of the word "well" to avoid telling Macduff the truth.

In the desert air, where no one could hear them.

MACDUFF: What is your news?
Is it about the general cause?
Or is it a private grief for one person alone?

ROSS: Every good person shares in the woe,
But the main part is about you alone.

MACDUFF: If the news is for me,
Do not keep it from me. Quickly let me have it.

ROSS: Do not let your ears despise my tongue forever,
For I shall fill them with the heaviest sound
That ever yet they heard.

MACDUFF: I can guess what you are going to say.

ROSS: Your castle was surprised; your wife and babes
Savagely slaughtered.
I cannot tell you any more details,
For I am afraid it would kill you to hear it.

(MACDUFF *stands there, speechless and in shock.*)

MALCOLM: Merciful heaven! Macduff, say something!
Give words to your sorrow.
The grief that does not speak
Whispers to the heart and makes it break.

MACDUFF: My children, too?

ROSS: Wife, children, servants, all
That could be found.

MACDUFF: And I wasn't even there!
My wife was killed, too?

ROSS: I have said so.

MALCOLM: Be comforted.
Let us cure this deadly grief by taking revenge.

MACDUFF: But Macbeth has no children.
   All my pretty ones? Did you say all? All?
   What, all my pretty children and their mother
   At one fell swoop?

MALCOLM: Get revenge for this like a man.

MACDUFF: I shall do so;
   But I must also feel it as a man.
   I cannot stop thinking about all those things
   That were most precious to me. Did heaven look on,
   And not come to their defense? It was all my fault,
   Because I wasn't there to stop it!
   May heaven take care of them now.

MALCOLM: Let this sharpen your sword; let grief
   Change to anger. Blunt not your heart; enrage it.

MACDUFF: Oh, if I could only cry like a woman
   And take revenge like a man. But, gentle heaven,
   Bring this fiend of Scotland face to face with me.
   Set Macbeth within my sword's length.
   If he escapes, may heaven forgive him!

MALCOLM: Your words are brave.
   Come, we shall go to King Edward.
   The army is ready. All we need is permission to leave.
   Macbeth is like fruit ripe on the tree,
   Ready for shaking. Receive what cheer you may,
   The night is long that never finds the day.

(ALL *exit.*)

Act 5

Scene 1

Dunsinane. A room in the castle. A DOCTOR *and a Waiting* GENTLEWOMAN *enter.*

DOCTOR: I have watched with you for two nights, but I can see no truth in your report. When was it she last walked?

GENTLEWOMAN: Since his Majesty went into the field with the army, I have seen her rise from her bed, throw her robe on, open her closet, take some paper out of it, fold it, write on it, afterwards seal it, and again return to sleep. She does all this while she is still fast asleep.

DOCTOR: This is not normal! Besides walking and the other things she does, what, if anything, have you heard her say?

GENTLEWOMAN: I have heard her say things that I would rather not report.

DOCTOR: You may tell me. It is proper that you should.

GENTLEWOMAN: I will not tell you or anyone else. I have no witness to back me up.

(LADY MACBETH *enters, carrying a candle.*)

Look, here she comes! That is just how she looks; see how she is fast asleep. Watch her. Stand close.

DOCTOR: How did she get that candle?

GENTLEWOMAN: Why, it was right next to her. She has light by her all the time. It is her command.

DOCTOR: Look, her eyes are open.

GENTLEWOMAN: Yes, but she cannot see what is going on around her.

DOCTOR: What is she doing now? Look how she rubs her hands.

GENTLEWOMAN: She always does that. It looks as if she is washing her hands. I have known her to continue doing that for fifteen minutes.

LADY MACBETH: After all this washing, there is still a spot.

DOCTOR: Listen! She speaks. I will write down what she says, so I can remember it better.

LADY MACBETH: Out, damned spot! Out, I say! One o'clock, two o'clock, now it's time to do it. We have nothing to be afraid of, for no one can accuse us now. Yet who would have thought the old man to have had so much blood in him?

DOCTOR: Did you hear that?

LADY MACBETH: The Thane of Fife had a wife; where is she now? What, will these hands never be clean? No more of that, my lord, no more of that. You'll ruin everything with your startled movements.

DOCTOR (*to* LADY MACBETH): What are you talking about? It seems that you know what you should not know.

GENTLEWOMAN: She has said what she should not say, I am sure of that. Heaven knows what she has known.

LADY MACBETH: Here's the smell of the blood still. All the perfumes of Arabia will not sweeten this little hand. Oh, oh, oh!

DOCTOR: What a sigh she makes! Her heart is heavy.

GENTLEWOMAN: I would not have such a heart in my body for anything!

DOCTOR: Well, well, well.

GENTLEWOMAN: Let us hope she will get well, sir.

DOCTOR: This disease is beyond my practice. Yet I have known some who have walked in their sleep and later died in a holy state in their beds.

LADY MACBETH: Wash your hands, and put on your robe. Do not look so pale. I tell you again—Banquo's buried. He cannot come out of his grave.

DOCTOR: What is she saying?

LADY MACBETH: To bed, to bed! There's a knocking at the gate. Come, come, come, come, give me your hand. What's done cannot be undone. To bed, to bed, to bed!

(LADY MACBETH *exits.*)

DOCTOR: Will she go to bed now?

GENTLEWOMAN: Immediately.

DOCTOR: Terrible stories are being told
About evil deeds that have been done here.
Unnatural deeds bring on unnatural troubles.
She needs more help than I know how to give her.
God. God, forgive us all! Look after her.
Take from her reach anything that could hurt her.
Keep your eyes on her. So, good night!
I dare not speak about what I think.

GENTLEWOMAN: Good night, good Doctor.

(BOTH *exit.*)

Scene 2

The country near Dunsinane. Drums sound. MENTEITH, CAITHNESS, ANGUS, LENNOX, *and* SOLDIERS *enter.*

MENTEITH: The English army is near, led on by Malcolm,
His uncle Siward, and the good Macduff.
The desire for revenge burns in them.
After what happened to them, even a dead man
Would want to join them in battle.

ANGUS: We shall meet them near the Forest of Birnam.
That is the way they are coming.

CAITHNESS: Is Donalbain with his brother?

LENNOX: No, sir, he is not. I have a list of all the men
Who are coming. There is Siward's son,
And many beardless men that
Claim they are old enough to fight.

MENTEITH: What is that tyrant Macbeth doing?

CAITHNESS: He is fortifying his castle, Dunsinane.
Some say that he is mad. Others, who don't hate him
As much, say that he is full of brave fury.
But it is certain that his cause is so evil
He does not behave as one who knows he is right.

ANGUS: Now he feels
His secret murders sticking on his hands.
Now small revolts happen every minute,
Reminding him of his own lack of loyalty to Duncan.
Those he commands obey him
Only because he commands it, not out of love.
Now he feels his title hang loose about him,
Like a giant's robe upon a small thief.

MENTEITH: No wonder he rules so badly.

Everything in him feels guilty for being there.

CAITHNESS: Well, we must march on
To give obedience where it is truly owed.
We will soon meet Malcolm, the medicine
That will cure Scotland and save our country.

LENNOX: Yes, we shall.
Let us now march toward Birnam Forest.

(ALL *exit, marching.*)

Scene 3

Dunsinane. A room in the castle. MACBETH, DOCTOR, *and* ATTENDANTS *enter.*

MACBETH: Bring me no more reports.
Till the Forest of Birnam moves to Dunsinane Hill,
I have nothing to fear. What is the boy Malcolm?
Was he not born of woman? The spirits that know
The future have told me this:
"None of woman born shall harm Macbeth."
So get out, false Thanes; go live in England!
My mind and heart shall never sag with doubt
Nor shake with fear.

(*A* SERVANT *enters.*)

What do you want, you silly goose?

SERVANT: There are 10,000—

MACBETH: Geese, villain?

SERVANT: Soldiers, sir.

MACBETH: Why are you afraid of that,
You cowardly boy. What soldiers, fool?

SERVANT: The English force, your Majesty.

MACBETH: Get out of here!

(SERVANT *exits.*)

> This coming fight will decide everything.
> I will either remain King, or lose my throne forever.
> I have lived long enough. My youth is over.
> Those things that should accompany old age—
> Such as honor, love, respect, many friends—
> I must not expect to have. Instead, I have men
> Who obey me because they fear me.

(MACBETH *calls out to his lieutenant.*)

> Seyton! Where are you?

(SEYTON *enters.*)

SEYTON: What is your gracious pleasure?

MACBETH: What news do you have?

SEYTON: My lord, all that I reported earlier
Has been confirmed.

MACBETH: I'll fight until my flesh is hacked
From my bones. Give me my armor.

SEYTON: It is not needed yet.

MACBETH: I'll put it on anyway.
Send out more horses; search the countryside.
Hang those that talk of fear. Give me my armor.
(*to the* DOCTOR) How is your patient, Doctor?

DOCTOR: Her body is not sick, my lord.
But her mind is troubled with problems
That keep her from rest.

MACBETH: Cure her of that.
Can you not heal a sick mind,
Take from the memory a deep sorrow?

Erase the heavy troubles of the brain,
And with some sweet medicine
Clean out the dangerous stuff
That weighs upon her heart.

DOCTOR: In such cases, the patient
Must heal himself.

MACBETH: Throw medicine to the dogs;
I'll have none of it.
Seyton, come and help me put my armor on.
Come on, Seyton, quickly.
Doctor, the Thanes are all leaving me. If you can,
Find out what disease is troubling Scotland.
Make my country healthy again.
If you do this, I will reward you well.

DOCTOR: My good lord, I would if I could.

MACBETH: Seyton, this piece of armor is on wrong.
Don't worry about it now. Bring it after me.
I have no need to fear death and pain
Till the Forest of Birnam come to Dunsinane.

DOCTOR (*aside*): If I were away from Dunsinane,
Free and clear,
No promise of reward could bring me here.

(ALL *exit.*)

Scene 4

Country near Birnam Wood. Drums. MALCOLM, OLD
SIWARD *and his* SON, MACDUFF, MENTEITH, CAITHNESS,
ANGUS, *and* SOLDIERS *enter.*

MALCOLM: Cousins, I hope the days are near at hand
When people can sleep safely in their beds.

MENTEITH: I am sure they are, sir.

SIWARD: What forest is this before us?

MENTEITH: It is the Forest of Birnam.

MALCOLM: Let every soldier cut himself a branch
    And hold it before him. In that way, we will
    Hide our great numbers and make it difficult
    For Macbeth's spies to count us.

SOLDIERS: It shall be done.

SIWARD: The only news we have heard is that
    The confident tyrant, Macbeth,
    Is still in Dunsinane. He will wait for us
    To come to him.

MALCOLM: That is his main hope, for he knows that
    It would be much easier for his men to desert him
    In the field than at the castle. No one serves him,
    Except those whose hearts are elsewhere.

MACDUFF: Let us not talk of the outcome of the fight
    Until after the battle.

SIWARD: The time approaches that will let us know
    What the true results will be.
    Trying to guess the outcome only tells us our hopes.
    Certain issues must be decided by actual blows,
    So let the battle begin.

(ALL *exit, marching.*)

Scene 5

Dunsinane. Within the castle. MACBETH, SEYTON, *and*
SOLDIERS *enter.*

MACBETH: Hang out our flags on the outer walls.
    The cry is still, "They come!" Our castle's strength
    Will laugh at their efforts to attack. Here let them lie

Till they die of starvation and fever.
If their army had not been increased by soldiers
Who deserted us, we might have met them
In hand-to-hand combat, and sent them home.

(*A cry of women is heard from within.*)

What is that noise?

SEYTON: It is the cry of women, my good lord.
I'll go find out what happened.

(SEYTON *exits.*)

MACBETH: I have almost forgotten the taste of fear.
In the past, my senses would have cooled
To hear a shriek like that,
And my hair would stand on end as if
Life were in it. I have been living with such horrors
That such a shriek cannot even affect me.

(SEYTON *enters.*)

What was that cry all about?

SEYTON: The Queen, my lord, is dead.

MACBETH: She would have died sooner or later,
But later would have been better.
Tomorrow, and tomorrow, and tomorrow,
Creeps in this petty[1] pace from day to day
To the last syllable of recorded time;
And all our yesterdays have shown fools
The way to dusty death. Out, out, brief candle!
Life's just a walking shadow, a poor player
That struts and frets his hour upon the stage
And then is heard no more. It is a tale

---

1. petty having little importance or value

Told by an idiot, full of sound and fury,
Signifying nothing.

(*A* MESSENGER *enters.*)

You came to say something; say it quickly.

MESSENGER: My lord, I should report what I saw,
But I do not know how to do it.

MACBETH: Just say it, sir.

MESSENGER: As I stood my watch upon the hill,
I looked toward Birnam, and I thought
The forest began to move.

MACBETH: You are a liar!

MESSENGER: Be angry with me only if it is not true.
It's less than three miles away;
You can see it coming: I say, a moving grove.[2]

MACBETH: If you are lying,
You shall be hanged from the nearest tree,
Till you die of starvation. If your words are true,
I do not care if you do the same to me.
I begin to doubt the words of the Vision
That lies like the truth:
"Macbeth shall never be conquered until
The Forest of Birnam comes to Dunsinane Hill."
And now, a forest comes toward Dunsinane.
Every man take up arms! Get ready to fight!
Ring the alarm bells! Come, ruin! Wind, rattle!
At least we'll die wearing armor, in battle!

(ALL *exit.*)

---

2. grove a group of trees standing together

Scene 6

Dunsinane. Before the castle. Drums sound. MALCOLM,
OLD SIWARD, MACDUFF, *and their* ARMY *enter. The*
SOLDIERS *hold branches.*

MALCOLM: Now we are near enough.
  Throw down your leafy screens
  And show yourselves to the enemy.
  (*to* OLD SIWARD) You, worthy uncle,
  Shall lead the first body of troops,
  Along with my cousin, your noble son.
  Worthy Macduff and I shall lead the others,
  According to our plan.

SIWARD: Fare you well.
  If we find the tyrant's army tonight,
  Let us be beaten, if we cannot fight.

MACDUFF: Make all our trumpets speak;
  Give them all breath,
  They announce the coming of blood and death.

(ALL *exit. Trumpets sound.*)

Scene 7

Another part of the field. MACBETH *enters.*

MACBETH: I feel like a bear tied to a stake;[3]
  I cannot run, but, bearlike, I must fight.
  What is he that was not born of woman?
  He is the one I must fear, nobody else.

(YOUNG SIWARD *enters.*)

---

3. a bear tied to a stake In bearbaiting, a favorite old English
  sport, a bear was tied to a stake and dogs were set loose to attack it.

YOUNG SIWARD: What is your name?

MACBETH: You would be afraid if you heard it.

YOUNG SIWARD: No, I would not.

MACBETH: My name is Macbeth.

YOUNG SIWARD: The devil himself could not say a name
　　More hateful to my ear.

MACBETH: Nor could he say a name more to be feared.

YOUNG SIWARD: You lie, hated tyrant.
　　With my sword, I'll prove it.

(They fight and YOUNG SIWARD *is killed.)*

MACBETH: You were born of woman.
　　But at swords I smile, all weapons I scorn,
　　If used by a man that's of a woman born.

(MACBETH *exits.* YOUNG SIWARD's *body is removed from the stage.* MACDUFF *enters.*)

MACDUFF: The noise was over here.
　　Tyrant, show your face.
　　If you are killed by anyone but me
　　The ghosts of my wife and children
　　Will haunt me forever.
　　I cannot strike at your soldiers, who fight
　　Only because they are hired to do so.
　　Either I find you, Macbeth,
　　Or else I shall put my sword away unused.
　　Judging by all the noise, you should be close.
　　Fortune, let me find him!
　　I ask for no more than that.

(MACDUFF *exits.* MALCOLM *and* OLD SIWARD *enter.*)

SIWARD: This way, my lord.

The castle has surrendered without fighting.
Our own noble Thanes are winning.
Victory declares itself yours,
And little is left to do.

MALCOLM: We have met with enemies
Who are fighting on our side.

SIWARD: Sir, enter the castle.

(ALL *exit.*)

Scene 8

Before Macbeth's castle. MACBETH *enters.*

MACBETH: Why should I kill myself with my own sword
Just because we are losing?
As long as I see any enemies living, the gashes
Would be better on them.

(MACDUFF *enters.*)

MACDUFF: Turn and face me, Macbeth!

MACBETH: Of all the men here, I have avoided you.
Please get back; my soul is much too heavy
With your family's blood already.

MACDUFF: I have no words to describe you;
My voice is in my sword! You are a bloodier villain
Than words could ever say!

(*They fight.*)

MACBETH: You are wasting your efforts.
It would be easier for you to cut the air
With your sword than to cut me.
I live a charmed life, which will not yield
To one born of a woman.

MACDUFF: Forget about your charmed life!
　Let the evil spirit whom you still serve
　Tell you this: Macduff was taken
　From his mother's womb prematurely.
　I was not born in the normal way.

MACBETH: Cursed be the tongue that tells me so,
　For it has made my courage fail!
　May those deceiving fiends no longer be believed.
　They speak to us in double meanings.
　I will not fight with you.

MACDUFF: Then give up, coward,
　And live to be a sideshow.
　We'll have your picture painted on a board
　And attached to a pole,
　As we do with our rarer monsters.
　Underneath, we shall write:
　"Here you may see the tyrant."

MACBETH: I will not give up,
　To kiss the ground before young Malcolm's feet
　And to be taunted by the peasants.
　Though Birnam Forest has come to Dunsinane,
　And you were not born of a woman,
　Yet I will fight to the end. Before my body,
　I hold my warlike shield. Fight on, Macduff,
　And cursed be he that first cries, "Stop, enough!"

(*They exit, fighting. Drums sound, and* MALCOLM, OLD
SIWARD, ROSS, THANES, *and* SOLDIERS *enter.*)

MALCOLM: I wish that none of our friends had died.

SIWARD: Some must die in battle. And yet,
　It seems that we had very few losses.

MALCOLM: Macduff is missing, and your noble son.

ROSS: My lord, your son was killed in battle.
He lived only until he was a man,
But like a man he died.

SIWARD: Then he is dead?

ROSS: Yes, and brought off the field.
If you measured your sorrow by his worth,
Then it would have no end.

SIWARD: Were his wounds on the front?

ROSS: Yes, on the front.

SIWARD: Well then, he died bravely,
Facing his enemy.
And so, God be with him!

(MACDUFF *enters, with* MACBETH's *head.*)

MACDUFF (*to* MALCOLM): Hail, King! Behold this,
The tyrant's cursed head. We are now free.
Hail, King of Scotland!

ALL: Hail, King of Scotland!

MALCOLM: I shall lose no time in rewarding all of you
For what you have done today.
My Thanes and kinsmen, from this day forth,
You are earls,[4] the first ones in Scotland.
We shall soon call our exiled friends back home,
And we shall bring to trial the cruel agents
Of this dead butcher and his fiendish queen,
Who, they say, took her own life.
So, thanks to all at once and to each one,
Whom we invite to see us crowned at Scone.

(ALL *exit.*)

---

4. **earls** an English title, not used in Scotland before this

SUMMARY OF PLAY

ACT 1

Near a battlefield in Scotland, Three Witches meet during a storm. They agree to meet again when the battle is over. Then they will meet Macbeth, a Scottish captain.

A sergeant reports to King Duncan. Macbeth and another captain, Banquo, have helped win the battle. To reward Macbeth for his brave acts on the field, Duncan gives him the title Thane of Cawdor.

That evening, the Three Witches greet Macbeth by his new title. They tell him that he will soon be king. They also tell Banquo that his sons and grandsons will be kings, but he will not be one himself. The Witches disappear. Messengers arrive to tell Macbeth that he is now Thane of Cawdor.

Duncan names his son Malcolm as his successor and informs Macbeth that he himself will be coming to Inverness, Macbeth's castle, for a visit.

Lady Macbeth reads a letter from her husband. He tells her about the Witches' prophecies. A messenger arrives to announce the King's visit. When Macbeth gets there, she tells him that Duncan will not live until morning. She tells Macbeth to leave all the details to her.

Duncan arrives and is welcomed.

Macbeth discusses the murder plan with Lady Macbeth. He is having second thoughts. She accuses him of being afraid to commit the crime.

ACT 2

Banquo and his son, Fleance, are in the courtyard after midnight. Macbeth enters. Macbeth and Banquo talk about the Witches' predictions.

After Lady Macbeth drugs Duncan's guards, Macbeth kills Duncan. Lady Macbeth smears the sleeping guards with blood. Knocking is heard from the south entry of the castle. Macbeth and Lady Macbeth go to wash the blood off their hands and to change into their nightclothes.

Macduff and Lennox are let in by the porter. They have come to awaken Duncan, at his earlier request. They discover the body. Macbeth kills Duncan's guards, blaming Duncan's death on them. Duncan's sons, Malcolm and Donalbain, flee.

Ross and Macduff decide that Duncan's sons paid the guards to kill their father.

ACT 3

Macbeth invites Banquo to a banquet. Banquo promises to be there. Macbeth arranges to have Banquo and Fleance killed on their way to the banquet.

Macbeth hints to his wife that soon Banquo and Fleance will pose no problems.

Three murderers, hired by Macbeth, attack Fleance and Banquo. Fleance escapes, and Banquo is murdered.

That evening, Macbeth and Lady Macbeth, as king and queen, welcome guests to a banquet. As everyone sits down, Macbeth sees a vision of Banquo's ghost. He speaks to it in such a way that his part in Banquo's death becomes clear. Lady Macbeth orders the guests to leave. She says that her husband is not himself.

Lennox and another lord talk about Macbeth's suspicious behavior. Macduff goes to England, where Duncan's son, Malcolm, has fled, in order to get help against Macbeth.

ACT 4

Macbeth visits the Three Witches and asks them about his future. They produce a series of visions that reveal the future in the form of riddles. After the Witches disappear, Lennox arrives. He tells Macbeth that Macduff has fled to England. Angry about this, Macbeth orders the murder of Macduff's family.

Murderers kill everyone at Macduff's castle.

In England, Malcolm and Macduff make plans to restore peace to Scotland. Ross arrives with news about the murder of Macduff's family. This makes Macduff's desire to overthrow Macbeth even stronger.

ACT 5

Lady Macbeth seems to have gone mad. She walks in her sleep.

As she does, she talks about blood on her hands.

Near Dunsinane, the forces led by Malcolm and Macduff get ready to attack.

Macbeth prepares for the attack. A doctor tells Macbeth that he can do nothing for Lady Macbeth.

Malcolm orders his men to hide behind branches cut from the trees of Birnam Wood.

Macbeth receives word that Lady Macbeth is dead. He also hears that Birnam Wood is moving toward Dunsinane. Remembering the vision's words, "None of woman born shall harm Macbeth," Macbeth still feels safe.

The forces against Macbeth arrive.

Macbeth kills young Siward in battle.

Macbeth finds out that Macduff was not born in the normal way. Therefore, the Witches' words do not apply to him. Macduff kills Macbeth, and Malcolm becomes king.

REVIEWING YOUR READING

ACT 1

FINDING THE MAIN IDEA

1. The prophecies of the Three Witches lead Macbeth and Lady Macbeth to

   (A) invite Duncan and the Thanes to a party (B) plot the murder of Duncan (C) believe that Macbeth has been seeing things (D) plan improvements for the commoners.

REMEMBERING DETAILS

2. Duncan rewards Macbeth for his

   (A) goodness (B) cooking (C) bravery (D) spying.

3. The Thane of Cawdor is executed for being a

   (A) thief (B) liar (C) coward (D) traitor.

4. The Witches tell Banquo that he will

   (A) be the father of kings (B) be a king (C) have a happy life (D) be murdered.

5. Duncan names _____ as his successor.

   (A) Donalbain (B) Malcolm (C) Macbeth (D) Banquo

DRAWING CONCLUSIONS

6. When Lady Macbeth says, "Yet I do fear your nature;/It is too full of the milk of human kindness/To go the fastest way," we can assume that

   (A) Macbeth drinks too much milk (B) Lady Macbeth is afraid of her husband (C) Macbeth moves too slowly (D) Macbeth is really a kind man.

7. Lady Macbeth gives the guards wine and liquor to

   (A) make them sleep through the murder (B) reward them (C) use it up (D) show her generosity.

8. When Lady Macbeth says that Duncan will never "see the sun again," she means that he will

   (A) be blind (B) be dead before morning (C) never leave the house (D) be put in prison.

98

USING YOUR REASON

9. Duncan wants to visit Macbeth's castle because

    (A) his wife is there, visiting Lady Macbeth   (B) he wants to honor Macbeth even more   (C) Lady Macbeth gives good parties (D) Inverness is more comfortable than Duncan's palace.

IDENTIFYING THE MOOD

10. Macbeth's mood in his soliloquy in Scene 7 that begins, "If it must be done…" can best be described as

    (A) unsure   (B) joyful   (C) confident   (D) silly.

THINKING IT OVER

11. Do you think Macbeth would have gone ahead with the murder if Lady Macbeth had not pushed him into it? Find evidence in the text to support your answer.

ACT 2

FINDING THE MAIN IDEA

1. The main thing that happens in this act is

    (A) Macbeth can't say "Amen"   (B) Macbeth kills Duncan (C) Macduff finds Duncan's body   (D) Lady Macbeth faints.

REMEMBERING DETAILS

2. The signal for Macbeth to kill Duncan is

    (A) an owl hooting   (B) a rooster crowing   (C) a bell being rung by his wife   (D) Duncan snoring.

3. Lady Macbeth goes back to Duncan's room to

    (A) see the body   (B) kill the guards   (C) clean it   (D) smear the guards with blood.

4. When the knocking is heard, Lady Macbeth tells her husband to

    (A) put on his hat   (B) answer the door   (C) put on his nightclothes   (D) put out the lights.

5. Macduff and Lennox come to Macbeth's castle because they

    (A) have instructions to wake Duncan at a certain time   (B) are lost   (C) are hungry   (D) are cold.

DRAWING CONCLUSIONS

6. Macbeth kills the guards because

    (A) they would have denied the murder   (B) they tried to kill him
    (C) Lady Macbeth told him to   (D) they tried to kill Malcolm.

7. Malcolm and Donalbain flee because they

    (A) think they might be suspected of the murder   (B) think they
    might be murdered next   (C) are tired of Scotland   (D) need a
    vacation.

USING YOUR REASON

8. Lady Macbeth can't kill Duncan herself because

    (A) she has no weapon   (B) she is too weak   (C) the guards stop
    her   (D) he reminds her of her father.

IDENTIFYING THE MOOD

9. The overall mood suggested by Macbeth's soliloquy beginning,
   "Is this a dagger which I see before me?" is one of

    (A) silliness   (B) horror   (C) happiness   (D) sleepiness.

THINKING IT OVER

10. After Duncan's murder, why does suspicion fall on Malcolm and
    Donalbain? Explain your answer.

11. In Scene 1, why do you think Banquo says that he "could not
    sleep"? What do you think has been keeping him awake?

12. Which person do you think is more disturbed by Duncan's
    murder—Macbeth or Lady Macbeth? Find evidence in the text to
    support your answer.

ACT 3

FINDING THE MAIN IDEA

1. The most important thing in this act is

    (A) the murder of Banquo   (B) Macbeth's meeting with the
    murderers   (C) Macduff going to England   (D) Lennox
    suspecting Macbeth.

REMEMBERING DETAILS

2. Before the feast, Banquo and Fleance go

    (A) for a walk   (B) horseback riding   (C) to sleep
    (D) to England.

3. Macbeth tells the murderers that Banquo

    (A) betrayed them   (B) killed Duncan   (C) is his brother (D) is a
    traitor.

4. Regarding the murder of Banquo, Lady Macbeth

    (A) plans the whole thing   (B) knows nothing about it   (C) tells
    the lords about it   (D) prevents it.

5. When Macbeth finds out that Fleance escaped, he

    (A) is glad   (B) doesn't really care   (C) sends bloodhounds out
    to find him   (D) is very upset.

DRAWING CONCLUSIONS

6. We can guess that the murderers are

    (A) good men who have been mistreated   (B) failures who blame
    their misfortune on others   (C) good fathers   (D) hard workers.

7. When Macbeth says to Lady Macbeth, "We are but young in such
    things," we can assume that

    (A) they are in their 20s   (B) he has plans for more evil deeds
    (C) they are under 40   (D) it is early in the evening.

USING YOUR REASON

8. The reason that Macbeth wants to have Fleance murdered is that

    (A) the Witches said Banquo would be the father of kings
    (B) Fleance is a traitor   (C) he just doesn't like him   (D) Fleance
    tried to kill Macbeth.

IDENTIFYING THE MOOD

9. Macbeth's soliloquy in Scene 1 that begins, "To be a king is
    nothing," creates a mood of

    (A) peace   (B) dissatisfaction   (C) joy   (D) courage.

THINKING IT OVER

10. Scene 5 shows that the lords are beginning to suspect Macbeth of

foul play. What do you think leads them to this belief? Use evidence from the text to support your answer.

11. What do you predict will happen to Macbeth and Lady Macbeth? Save your answer and compare it to what happens during the next two acts.

ACT 4

FINDING THE MAIN IDEA

1. The main thing that happens in this act is
(A) Macbeth has Macduff's family killed (B) a vision of Banquo rises from the Witches' cauldron (C) Macduff and Malcolm have a meeting (D) the Witches disappear.

REMEMBERING DETAILS

2. The first vision tells Macbeth that
(A) he has three ears (B) he should beware of Macduff
(C) the trees will march (D) Banquo will return.

3. The second vision tells Macbeth that
(A) his wife will die (B) he will be defeated in battle (C) none of woman born will harm him (D) Banquo's sons will be kings.

4. The third vision tells Macbeth that he will
(A) not be defeated until Birnam Wood comes to Dunsinane hill
(B) kill Fleance in battle (C) lose a great battle to Malcolm's forces (D) have many children.

5. Lennox comes to tell Macbeth that
(A) Lady Macduff is dead (B) Lady Macbeth is dead
(C) Macduff has fled to England (D) the Witches are gone.

DRAWING CONCLUSIONS

6. Lady Macduff is angry with her husband for
(A) staying out too late (B) not writing (C) going to too many parties (D) leaving his family unprotected.

7. Because Macduff leaves Scotland, we can assume that he
(A) does not think that Macbeth will harm his family (B) has friends to visit (C) wants to travel (D) wants to get some gifts for his family.

USING YOUR REASON

8. The messenger who comes to warn Lady Macduff does not stay long because

    (A) he knows the murderers are on their way   (B) he has other plans   (C) he isn't invited   (D) Lady Macduff asks him to leave.

IDENTIFYING THE MOOD

9. Macduff's immediate reaction to the news about his family can best be described as one of

    (A) relief   (B) gratitude   (C) shock   (D) violence.

THINKING IT OVER

10. Why do you think Malcolm tells Macduff so many lies about himself? Find evidence in the text to support your answer.

11. Why do you think it takes Ross so long to tell Macduff the bad news about his family? Explain your answer.

ACT 5

FINDING THE MAIN IDEA

1. The main thing that happens in this act is that

    (A) Lady Macbeth walks in her sleep   (B) Macbeth is defeated and Malcolm becomes king   (C) soldiers march, holding branches (D) Lady Macbeth dies.

REMEMBERING DETAILS

2. When Lady Macbeth walks in her sleep, she carries

    (A) a candle   (B) a book   (C) a dagger   (D) a wash basin.

3. The forces against Macbeth meet near

    (A) a heath   (B) Inverness   (C) Birnam Wood   (D) a lake.

4. When Macbeth and Young Siward meet in battle,

    (A) Young Siward runs away   (B) Macbeth is wounded
    (C) Macbeth is killed   (D) Young Siward is killed.

DRAWING CONCLUSIONS

5. Siward concludes that his son died bravely because

    (A) wounds on the front mean that he was not running away from a fight   (B) he knows that his son was brave   (C) a witness reports on the fight   (D) his son leaves a note.

6.   After Lady Macbeth's sleepwalking scene, we can assume that
(A) she will get better soon   (B) the doctor is not doing his job
(C) she feels guilty about the murders   (D) the gentlewoman will soon quit her job.

USING YOUR REASON

7.   The reason that the doctor cannot help Lady Macbeth is that
(A) methods of helping the mentally ill have not been developed yet   (B) he is not very smart   (C) she refuses his treatment
(D) Macbeth tells him not to.

IDENTIFYING THE MOOD

8.   Malcolm's last speech creates a mood of
(A) happiness   (B) sorrow   (C) horror   (D) shock.

THINKING IT OVER

9.   Why does Macbeth's fight with Young Siward reinforce his belief in the Witches' prophecies? Use evidence from the text to support your answer.

10. Do you think Macbeth is courageous in the end? Why or why not?

11. Do you think Malcolm will be a good king? Explain your answer.